Brave, moving, and poignant. An important story, honestly and beautifully told, of pain transformed into hope. The world is in great need of courageous voices like DeMuth's.

TOSCA LEE, author of Christy-award finalist *Demon: A Memoir* and *Havah: The Story of Eve*

This gifted memoirist writes like a woman at the well: *Thin Places* reads like rivers of living water. With her incantatory language, Mary DeMuth describes both the burden of suffering and the weightlessness of redemption. If you're carrying past wounds, read this book. It will change your life.

SIBELLA GIORELLO, Christy-award-winning novelist

Author Mary DeMuth has lived up to readers' expectations of exquisite writing from an exceptional author. She has also opened herself and allowed readers to see inside—all the hurts, disappointments, violations—in order to escort the readers on a painfully joyful journey to healing. A rare memoir from one of the best writers of our time!

KATHI MACIAS, author of more than thirty books, including *Beyond Me* and *Mothers of the Bible Speak to Mothers of Today*

Mary DeMuth's latest work, *Thin Places*, is a true example of courage. Seemingly without holding back, Mary has exposed to herself and to those who read her work the thin places of her life where God showed up. In doing so, she helps others realize the thin places of their own lives and how God moves in and around them.... Every word is beautifully penned and sincerely written.

EVA MARIE EVERSON, author of *Things Left Unspoken*

Thin Places is strong medicine for every reader who ever felt hopelessly damaged or desperately inadequate. Mary DeMuth shows the way back to innocence and wonder. There are too few books like this, too few authors so courageous.

KATHLEEN POPA, author of *To Dance in the Deser*

Women today are hungry for words that narrate life as it really is. We're dying to know we're not alone. In *Thin Places*, Mary DeMuth tells the truth about loss, pain, sin, and redemption. *Thin Places* sets the table for readers to see, hear, and taste God's unfailing nearness. Enjoy the feast.

> MARGOT STARBUCK, author of *The Girl in the Orange Dress: Searching for a Father Who Does Not Fail*

Mary's memoir is real and raw and beautifully written. She shows the ugliness of humanity and the beauty of redemption. I laughed and I cried, and it made me want to be a better writer. *Thin Places* will be put in my waiting room to help others find hope and see that Jesus loves and God is present, even in the loneliest and most horrific circumstances.

> LESLIE VERNICK, LCSW, licensed counselor and international speaker, author of *The Emotionally Destructive Relationship*

Of the many gifts God has lavished on Mary DeMuth, one I admire most is her courage to go to the raw places and help us look for God's presence there. In this unflinching look at her own story, DeMuth offers us vulnerability and hope that God is relentless in His love even when we doubt it the most.

> CATHERINE CLAIRE LARSON, author of *As We Forgive: Stories of Reconciliation from Rwanda* and senior writer and editor for *BreakPoint*

With brutal honesty, Mary paints a vivid picture of the cruel blows life delivers to all of us. But her ability to shine light on what God does through pain and difficulty is a revelation of His infinite love and grace. *Thin Places* reminded me that beauty really does come from ashes. I'm not the same after reading this book.

> TOM DAVIS, CEO, Children's HopeChest, and author of *Red Letters: Living a Faith that Bleeds*

In *Thin Places*, Mary DeMuth gently takes your fingers in her hand and guides them across the breathtaking mosaic that is her life. I felt every sharp edge, each rough and aching path, and marveled at the startling beauty of her brokenness. Savor this book."

CLAUDIA MAIR BURNEY, author of *Zora and Nicky: A Novel in Black and White*

When I get my official copy of *Thin Places*, I'm thinking of having it bound in a gold-embossed bonded-leather cover with gilded page edges. Yes, it's that much of a treasure to be cherished for a lifetime of reading. I'm tempted to request a zipper for its custom binding. That would symbolize DeMuth's success at unlocking and interlacing her innermost story and soul with the Scriptures in a way that opens us all to the thickness of "thin."

LEONARD SWEET, Drew University, George Fox Evangelical Seminary, www.sermons.com

I've never read a more authentic and real account of trials turned to hope. *Thin Places* will open your eyes to the beauty of "seeing" through those heart-wrenching times and grasping our Savior's hand. DeMuth reminds us that our great God sees us where we are, and He loves us unconditionally. Thank you, Mary, for sharing the depths of your heart with us. This book is a treasure.

KIMBERLEY WOODHOUSE, author of *Welcome Home: Our Family's Journey to Extreme Joy* and seen on *Extreme Makeover: Home Edition*

Thin Places, a memoir by Mary DeMuth, has captured my heart. Mary is a fun and happy person, so her vulnerability in telling this painful story of childhood abuse is deeply moving. Mary writes beautifully, even poetically, and leaves the reader with a sense of hope and courage.

HEATHER GEMMEN WILSON, bestselling author and international speaker *www.heathergemmen.com*

Thin Places

a memoir

Mary E. DeMuth

ZONDERVAN®

ZONDERVAN.com/
AUTHORTRACKER
follow your favorite authors

ZONDERVAN

Thin Places
Copyright © 2010 by Mary E. DeMuth

This title is also available as a Zondervan ebook. Visit www.zondervan.com/ebooks.

This title is also available in a Zondervan audio edition. Visit www.zondervan.fm.

Requests for information should be addressed to:

Zondervan, *Grand Rapids, Michigan 49530*

Library of Congress Cataloging-in-Publication Data

DeMuth, Mary E., 1967–
    Thin places: a memoir / Mary DeMuth.
      p. cm.
    Includes bibliographical references.
    ISBN 978-0-310-28418-5 (softcover)
    1. DeMuth, Mary E., 1967– 2. Christian biography—United States. I. Title.
BR1725.D4A3   2009
277.3'082092—dc22   2009020798

---

09 10 11 12 13 14 15 • 24 23 22 21 20 19 18 17 16 15 14 13 12 11 10 9 8 7 6 5 4 3 2 1

To Jeanne Damoff who dances
in Jacob-shaped thin places with joy.
And to Pam LeTourneau who sings
and marvels in new thin places.

Contents

Note: Some names have been changed
and situations altered to protect privacy.

Amazing Grave

Growing up, I find myself housed in a scrawny sort of body — legs thin as broomsticks, interrupted by knees so knobby they bang into each other when I walk. My doctor makes me drink whole milk so I'll fatten up. Kids use words like *rail*, *string bean*, or *stick* to describe me.

I, myself, am a thin place.

The Celts define a *thin place* as a place where heaven and the physical world collide, one of those serendipitous territories where eternity and the mundane meet. Thin describes the membrane between the two worlds, like a piece of vellum, where we see a holy glimpse of the eternal — not in digital clarity, but clear enough to discern what lies beyond.

Thin places are snatches of holy ground, tucked into the corners of our world, where, if we pay very close attention, we might just catch a glimpse of eternity. Legend has it that thin places are places for pilgrims, where ghostlike echoes of those gone before can be felt and heard, where the Ancients whisper their wisdom near the ruins of a church or the craggy outcropping of a rock. In this way, a thin place is an ancient doorway to the fairy-tale netherworld — a fanciful notion that children embrace and adults find preposterous.

Maybe it's my own imagination that hopes for real thin places on this earth. I'm a storyteller, after all, prone to wander in make-believe worlds. I'd like to believe in portals to eternity — Narnia doors beckoning me onward and upward. Even so, I'm broadening the metaphor a bit. Thin places are snatches of time, moments really, when we sense God intersecting our world in tangible, unmistakable ways. They are aha moments, beautiful realizations, when the Son of God bursts through the hazy fog of our monotony and shines on us afresh.

He has come near to my life. I will tell you how.

When I learn of my grandmother's cancer, how it ravages her body though it spares her mind, I fly out to visit, knowing it may be our last time to clasp hands on earth. The feisty woman stares back at me, her body visibly shorter, her eyes holding a flicker of sass but mostly sadness. I want the evangelical gumption others furiously possess to share with my grandmother the beauty of Jesus with a flurry of perfectly scripted words. But the words don't spill out. Instead, I play cards with her. We reminisce about our summers together, laughing. I enter her world, hold her hand, tell her I love her.

I accompany her to Bingo, enduring the choking smoke and grilling despair that seeps into the Bingo Hall. While the caller shouts out letters and numbers, and folks near death stamp card upon card, I know that if Jesus walked the earth today, He'd hang out in a Bingo Hall, loving on folks whose only hope is a five-hundred-dollar jackpot.

I panic before I am about to fly home. Billy Graham shouts in my conscience, *You have to share the gospel. You have to share the gospel.* I pray, keep quiet. I listen to the Holy Spirit's sweet voice. *Pray for her*, He says.

"Do you mind if I pray for you before I leave?" I ask.

"Not at all." Her voice sounds small, needy. "I'd like that."

I pray that she will understand Jesus' winsome love for her, that she will be relieved of pain, that she'll know beyond a doubt that God sees her there, hurting. I ask Him to please shoulder her burdens, whatever they may be. When *amen* leaves my lips, my grandmother's shiny eyes stare back at me. The Scripture comes to mind about doing things unto the least of these and how, in serving those who were needy, I serve Jesus Himself.

I cry.

She cries.

We embrace.

When I leave, I am haunted. Why didn't I spell out the entirety of the gospel? What if she wanted to know? I pray again when I arrive home, clearly sensing God wants me to write her a letter, share my heart about my life, Jesus, all the healing He's done inside me, the forgiveness He offers even now. Though I feel like I've flunked Evangelism 101, I send the letter.

A little later I call her.

"Thank you for the letter," she wheezes.

"You're welcome," I reply, still hesitant.

"You don't understand," she says. "I love that letter. I read it over and over again. Thank you for writing it."

I choke out an "I love you" and hang up.

A few days later she lets out her last breath.

I stand above my grandmother's grave, a gaping, muddy hole in the Ohio earth. The casket holding the shell of her body teeters on top as the wind blows through me, around me. Barren trees reach stark limbs to the sky as if to beckon it to send sunshine.

I remember Bingo, the prayer, the letter. I have no idea if my grandmother met Jesus, but in that sacred silence, I am stirred to sing Amazing Grace over the coffin, though the wind blows and the trees creak branches together.

Amazing grace, how sweet the sound that saved a wretch like me.

Sobs warble my voice just as others join in.

A thin place, this Ohio graveyard. I can nearly see Jesus' smile as I catch a paper-thin glimpse of heaven on the November breeze. God's fingerprints are everywhere—in the sacred intersection of melancholy and joy. I feel like Jacob, himself akin to thin places. Head pillowed on a rock, Jacob dreams crazy ladder dreams where angels dance up and down, to and from God's presence. God shouts covenant words in the dream, words establishing Jacob as a patriarch and promising Jacob His presence. Jacob wakes up and utters these words: "Surely the Lord is in this place, and I did not know it" (Genesis 28:16 NASB).

Surely God is in the nooks and crannies of my life, stooping to earth to woo me. Sometimes I recognize Him, but usually I continue on the mundane path, not realizing a breath of a veil exists between the Almighty and myself. Margaret Becker's song "Cave It In" beautifully captures this:

> *I know the wall between us*
> *Is just paper-thin*
> *Why can't I, why can't I,*
> *Why can't I just cave it in?*
> *So porous these walls may be*
> *But I'm still clawing at the seams.*[1]

That's me. I live in the midst of holy moments, yet only in retrospect do I really see them. I claw at the seams of life, questioning God's ways, seldom realizing that if I'd stop clawing, I would capture new glimpses of Him through the thin places. God woos me from behind the veil through the tragedies, beauties, surprises, simplicities, and snatches of my life I might overlook.

I once was lost, but now am found, was blind, but now I see.

1

Studebaker

At four years old, long before seat belt laws, I crouch down on the floor of my father's dying Studebaker, pressing my left eye to the rusted floor where a convenient hole the size of my kneecap beckons. From time to time I look up from the floor, spying Jim — I never call him father — who wears a thrift-store cap over a bald head, dark brown fringe curls spilling out. It's the way our weekend visits go, an endless supply of quirky adventures with Jim at the helm. He nods at the hole, encouraging me with his smile to watch the street. I notice the wrinkles around his eyes.

I hover again over the hole while gray cement speeds past, blocks and miles whirring beneath my rapt gaze. I glimpse something of eternity — the ongoing universe passing me by, slowing to stop when Jim applies pressure to the brake. Later, when I share this memory, well-meaning adults spoil it by launching into a diatribe about how I could've lost an eye, wondering why in the world Jim didn't have any sense.

Eye to the Studebaker's rusting floor, I don't know God. Something in my preschool chest longs for a God who controls the rush of the street below, who holds the world's speed steady or brings it to an abrupt halt by applying pressure to a brake.

One ordinary fifth grade day, I am doing something rudimental like fractions or spelling or reading when the secretary's voice blares over the intercom, "Will Mary please come to the office right away?" The undercurrent of alarm in her voice startles me. I pick up my things and leave the classroom. I meander, somehow knowing that at the end of the outdoor walkway a terribly dark secret will be revealed and my life will never be the same.

I walk alone down the hall, noticing the brick patterns, counting my steps. Nearly to the office, the thought occurs to me: My father has died. I'm not sure how or why I know this. Perhaps the brick-lined hallway is a thin place where the Almighty whispers me a tender warning. As soon as I see my mother's face, I know.

In our idling green Datsun, parked with its nose facing the office, my mother puts words to my intuitions. "Your father is dead."

Because my mom has married twice more since being married to Jim, I feel the need to clarify. Which father? Jim who I visit every other weekend, whose tall, lanky frame I inherited? My first stepdad who took apart engines in our living room? Or my current stepfather who recently married my mom? I know in my gut who it is. Still I ask, "Which one?"

"Jim," she says.

My mom doesn't know what to do about grief, doesn't know how to console a ten-year-old in shock. She does not touch me. Instead she drives directly to Jafco, an electronics store of the 1970s. Pocket calculators are the newest thing.

"Pick one," she says, her eyes wet, her arms crossing her chest like armor. So I touch the small metal buttons of a calculator and hand it to her. The clerk puts it in a sack, hands it to me. I know

I'll be the first kid in my class to own one—the first kid with a pocket calculator and no father.

Jim's second wife is a widow now, with a bulging belly. Their daughter is born after he leaves earth, both of us fatherless.

After my father's death, I have a recurring dream that Jim lives in Africa and, although he misses me, he is happy there, tending gardens and constructing huts half a world away. I try to grab for his hand in the dreams, but he smiles until the wrinkles around his eyes fade to black nothingness.

Why do I dream Jim lives in Africa? Because no one gives me a satisfactory reason why or how he died. "An accident in the home," they say. Grown-ups whisper when I enter rooms, shoot me looks of pity. So I invent a story—a story I still use today when I feel someone's being particularly nosey. "My father fell down a flight of stairs in his home, hit his head on the cement, and bled to death." It seems logical. The steps of his Craftsman bungalow are steep, leading to the dank basement. I see the cement landing, put two and two together, and devise this viable story. It helps me endure the years until I discover the truth.

I dream this way because of Jim's closed casket. I sit near the front of the church where his coffin looms, large and cold. I remember very little about the day other than hymn singing and everyone wearing black. Faceless people hug me tight while tears run races down their cheeks. My father's widow has a hollow look, her pregnant belly nearly ready to give birth. For that day, people love me. Lavish attention on me. Hold me close. Whisper nearby. But it isn't long until I face school again where the meanest teacher of my elementary career awaits me. She scolds me once for what she thinks is cheating, sending me into the hall. "I used to feel sorry for you because your dad died, but you should be over it by now," she hisses. I come home to an empty house, do my homework, eat dinner, watch TV, and then cry myself to sleep right before I dream of Jim happy in Africa, all because I never see proof that he really died.

When I walk to school alone, I look behind me, worrying a stranger will reach out from nowhere and strangle me. I run from invisible chasers. I lock the back door behind me when I huff in from school. I am convinced I am next. If God's capricious finger has circled the fast-moving world and landed on my father's bald head, surely He'll summon me.

So I pray.

It's a strange thing to equate my longing for God with the death of Jim. Jim's casket makes me pray. Some primordial hunger inside me needs another Jim — someone to clutch me to his chest and tell me everything is going to be all right. That Jim, I hope, will be God. Late at night, with covers over my head because I still fear the boogeyman even at ten, I send little messages heavenward.

God, if You're there, speak to me.

God, do You love me?

God, help me to be happy.

God, I need a hug.

Some nights I can nearly hear His whispers, if I crane my neck just so, as I stay cocooned in the thin place beneath my covers.

Today I struggle knowing God "loves me and has a wonderful plan for my life." I seek Him everywhere — in my insatiable need for approval from others, in my "Do you love me?" pleas to my husband, in the dark places of my mind where I convince myself I'm a worthless mess and, therefore, unworthy of meriting the affection of the Almighty. Sometimes I'm still that little girl fighting against the grief of the world, longing for a snatch of light in the midst of dark days. I no longer pull the covers over my head—an indication that meeting Jesus twenty-four years ago spurred something cataclysmic in my heart that is still unfolding. He stoops to the level beside my bed, pulls away the covers, and sets me free.

Sometimes it seems verses in the Bible were written only for me. It's like the Holy Spirit, dictating words to scribes and prophets and shepherds, one day stops, smiles, thinks of me, and says, "Hey, write this down. Two thousand years from now, Mary will need to read this. This one's for her."

So Paul listens and writes these words. Just for me. (And maybe for you too.):

> For consider your calling, brethren [sisteren!], that there were not many wise according to the flesh, not many mighty, not many noble; but God has chosen the foolish things of the world to shame the wise, and God has chosen the weak things of the world to shame the things which are strong, and the base things of the world and the despised God has chosen, the things that are not, so that He may nullify the things that are, so that no man may boast before God.
>
> 1 Corinthians 1:26–29 NASB

I am not wise. But God chooses me anyway.
I am not mighty. But God chooses me anyway.
I am not of noble birth. But God chooses me anyway.
I am foolish. But God chooses me anyway.
I am weak. But God chooses me anyway.
I am base. But God chooses me anyway.
I am despised. But God chooses me anyway.

I am nothing. But God chooses me anyway.

I picture Him watching from heaven as I press my eye socket to the floor of Jim's Studebaker, watching God's chaotic world spin beneath me. "That one," He shouts to the heavenlies. "That raggedy one. I choose her because she knows her lack, because she knows her insatiable need for a father. Someday she'll cling to me." As I trace my fifth-grade hand over the brick wall leading to the office, He knows I am about to embark on a journey of fatherlessness, enduring the gaping hole that comes from a longing unfulfilled.

At nearly sixteen years old, I finish the journey I started under the Studebaker's floor mat. I hear about Jesus from Young Life leaders who love me — how Jesus chats with ordinary folks, goes fishing, heals bleeding women (oh, how my heart bleeds), and guffaws the religious pious. I fall in love with Jesus when I realize He commands the wind and the seas yet stoops to love the likes of me — a girl who wants to take her life, to rid the world of herself. He is the One I've been muttering prayers to under the cover of my bedspread. It is like having the President of the United States — someone far away and terribly important — turn up at my doorstep, entourage in tow, and take me to McDonald's for lunch. And order me a Big Mac and fries.

Under a blanket of stars that twinkle one icy night, I weep a prayer.

Jesus, can it really be true? That You love me? And want to be with me? Come into my life, then. Take me over. I'm a mess. I hope You don't regret it.

I cry the entire weekend, wetting my face, my pillow, my clothes with bottled up tears. It feels like Jesus is scrubbing me clean. Not the kind of washing you get from an overzealous grandmother bent on scouring the germs away, but the cleansing of a gentle stream, flowing over and through my parched soul.

Jesus washes me that night with my own tears. Or are they His?

But as the Psalmist so aptly writes, "Those who sow in tears shall reap with joyful shouting" (Psalm 126:5 NASB). My journey begins wide-eyed over a rusty hole. It continues when Jesus washes me in tears. And it marches forward still—after a quarter-of-a-century-long pilgrimage where joyful shouting comes and goes to the rhythm of this crazy, fickle life. I've come full circle, the wife of a man who is a doting father, who loves his kids well. And by some strange twist of God-irony, He gives me a daughter, my last, who looks just like me, and whose birthday, on some years, lands on Father's Day:

> *Two come by, year by year*
> *At least for the last nine*
> *When sometimes they collide*
> *Birth shaking hands with Death,*
> *Death not returning the favor*
>
> *Father's Day is never easy*
> *For the fatherless*
> *Half-orphaned, starved to the bone*
> *For Daddy love*
> *No man can fill*
>
> *Thirty years is a terrible lifetime*
> *To weave through days*
> *Without his hand*
> *His words*
> *His I love yous*

Nine years ago, she yowled hello
To her Daddy
So alive, she bawled and bawled
He held her
I melted
Crumbled

I will not know
What my daughter
Wears like a birthright
Around her heart
Her daddy's love

But I can taste it
I can see it
I can marvel
From the sidelines of parenthood

God's father-heart knew
I needed resurrection
Julia's life on my day of sorrow
Joy mingled with my gaping heart
United in her

Strange how life
Can't be helped
Or hindered
Even when Death snatches
Fathers away

Resurrection is always
The answer to grief
New life, new yowls, new hopes
Mingled with

The life that was,
Old tears,
Old cynicisms

Thank You kindly
For the juxtaposition,
Jesus of the resurrection,
The One who weeps on Father's Day
Alongside me

Who pulled His beard
While the world ripped His flesh
And His father died to Him
In that terrible moment
History hinged upon

You understand resurrection
Invented it
Wove it into my life
On Father's Day
When my daughter
Cried her way into my arms

There's agony in that poem I do not allow myself to wallow in
—that empty place in my heart an earthly father will never fill.
Sitting across from some dear friends at dinner, the husband tells
the story of how he took his daughter on a trip to visit a college
campus. She didn't like the college immediately, which gave them
time together to do other things. He does what a loving father
does—helps his daughter find a college. Because he loves her.
In the midst of his recounting, my daddy-ache comes back. My
father never goes on college visits, never meets the man I marry,
never walks me down the aisle, never frolics with his grandchil-
dren. It's an injury that never seems to heal.

I am Jacob in times like this. Wrestling with God over my lack of a father, He injures me so I limp. The limp reminds me of God's God-ness and my frailty—the most humbling thin place. Yet it's this daddy-less thin place that reminds me that He is big enough to fill the need I've buried inside. Though I ache and will probably always carry a limp, I'm thankful the injury leads me back to Him.

2

Mary Jane

"Give this to your stepdad," the twenty-something snickers. Clad in the uniform of the early seventies — ripped jeans and a ratty T-shirt — he shoves a joint my way.

"Why?" I ask.

He laughs again. He and his friend exchange a knowing look. He bends low, grabs my five-year-old attention. "It's oregano," he says. "It's a funny trick, don't you think?" He waves the mock joint in my face, then puts it in my hand.

I'm all too aware of the realities of pot. Marijuana. Dope. Mary Jane. Hash. Hashish. It grows beautifully in my stepdad's closet under the hum of buzzing lamps. I think it is a pretty plant, vibrant green. Years later when I walk by Koffee Houses in Amsterdam, I am transported back to the little white house with that sweet, sickly smell I'll never forget.

I watch my parents' friends roll joints — as they pull out a coffee can, pinch the browning weed between two fingers, and drop it into a rectangle of see-through paper. They lick the envelope-like adhesive strip at one end, sealing the cylinder of dope. Lighters and matches flicker to life while groups of friends hold joints in joint clips, hissing in smoke. Others press the marijuana into pipes and bongs—a strange vocabulary for a five-year-old—their eyes turning to slits. They lean backward, looking at the ceiling. Smiles cross lips with each inhale.

Sometimes I slink away into my room when parties escalate. Even so, my bedroom is the one passageway to the bathroom, so I never escape the people lighting up, blowing smoke, smiling, singing, and shouting. I take to pulling the covers over my head, pressing the knuckles of each index finger into my ears and humming flower-child songs to keep the mayhem at bay. I shake sometimes. I press my body to the very end of the bed, hugging the wall, keeping as far away as I can from the party just feet away. I stay death-still, hoping no one notices me.

Other times I'm in the living room. Laughter echoes up the coved ceilings of the little white house. Some adults stagger. All of them swear. Smoke curls to the ceiling as a joint is passed in a circle, a roach clip holding the smoldering stick. Partygoers get so high they pass the joint to me.

"Come on. You'll have the time of your life," one slurs, his face near mine. He blows smoke in my face.

I cough.

I look at the smoldering joint. One end is red, the other soggy from all the mouths that kissed it. I smell it. Watch how the small white stick makes the adults sentimental and hungry. I say no. Not loud so others will hear and start making a game of getting the five-year-old stoned. I simply transfer the roach clip to the next adult and walk out of the room.

I find baggies of the oregano-like substance around the house. I know what marijuana seeds look like. Little white rolling papers slip into everything, ironic flakes of manna littering the floor of my little white house.

A trip to the country is a blurry reminder of the power of

marijuana. The log cabin sits on a hill, a wide, green field below it. The hippies there don't believe in The Man, so to stick it to Him, they are off the grid—no electricity or central heat. They light their cabin with kerosene lanterns, heat the interior with chopped, gnarled wood in a potbellied stove at the cabin's center. Bare-chested men sport long, bushy sideburns and wavy hair that dances below strong shoulders. Women weave crowns out of daisies to wear over stick-straight hair, parted in the middle.

I sleep with the hippie children, a passel of kids I meet during our sojourn at the cabin in the woods. We crowd and fight for floor space, bed space, sleep space, all the while smelling burning weed. Our parents laugh and dance and sway and inhale while we fend for ourselves.

My mom has an allergic reaction to a bug bite. She is swinging on a hammock on the front porch of the cabin, a bandage over her eye. She is pale. Why I fear she will die is a mystery to me, but I feel it in my gut. She is my anchor in this sea of stoned hippies, and I worry what will happen to me if she stops breathing.

She breathes.

Blessedly breathes.

And I'm safe, for now.

In the early days of adolescence, I find a stash. In the midst of wanting desperately to escape my life, I figure I'll see what all the hoopla is about. Maybe smoking a joint will provide a way to cope with life rather than replaying my desire to end my life. Maybe it will make me smile. I pinch the dried leaves between fingers, lifting them to my nose. That smell, that sugary, earthy smell. I shove the pinch into the barrel of a small pipe. I try to light the stuff, then cough and inhale smoke. Though I never try cigarettes, I try Mary Jane. Or it tries me. And finds me wanting. No ecstasy. No peace. No head bent back to the ceiling, a smile gracing my face. Just lots of coughing and a horrible sense of guilt.

I have a visceral reaction to anything smacking of cocaine, marijuana, and various sundry drugs. I spend my adolescence trying to avoid them. I don't go to parties. I look the other way in college. I avoid people who indulge. I'm terrified. Because I know how these things go. Drugs take away folks' sensibilities and inhibitions. Make them act stupid. Make them exploit children. Make them neglect. Panic isn't the right word to describe how seeing drugs makes me feel. It's not strong enough. Not violent enough.

During my college days, when I'm trying to listen to the prompting of the Holy Spirit, I decide I should pick up hitchhikers. What better way to witness to people in need than to pick them up and share Jesus? It sounds noble, but it certainly was not wise. I try it once. A woman stands in the middle of a major intersection, waving her arms wildly. I figure she's in need. I roll down my window and ask where she wants to go.

She yells at me, her eyes familiar with that crazed look. Something has taken her over. She sways on one foot, then the next. I panic. I roll up my window, but I can still hear her cursing, shaking her fist at a gray sky, spewing colorful vocabulary my direction. I speed away, heart pounding.

Battling kidney stones at thirty, I am rushed to the hospital. A shaggy-headed male nurse gives me a crooked smile. He has pushed an entire syringe of Demerol into my vein, enough for a person twice my size. I am fighting tigers. They're snarling in my face, taking swipes at me, roaring. They're as real as my breath, which now comes in shallow hyperventilation.

"Hey, don't worry about it," he says. "Relax and enjoy the trip. This is the best part. Don't you like being stoned?"

Though I cannot form words in the haze of the Demerol glut, I want to scream, "This is precisely why I never got stoned, Mr. Crazy Nurse Man. This feeling. This chaotic, out-of-control feeling."

At the airport, a willowy woman breezes by me, then sits on the chair between me and a man. I am waiting for my luggage. She must be thirty, dark hair pulled severely back, her speech slurred. She has the smile of the crazy nurse man, the wild-eyed look of the hitchhiker. She carries one of those metal briefcases. She drops it with a thud on the tiled floor.

"Hi," she says, loud enough for the entire baggage claim to hear. "I'm so sick of this." She exhales, long and slow. "I'm a makeup artist." The sunglasses on her head drop behind her so she tries to fetch them; but she can't, so she grabs my hand and shouts a few expletives. I can see she isn't going to be able to locate her missing glasses, so I retrieve them from behind the seat and hand them to her.

She calls someone on her cell phone and swears some more. "I don't know where I am," she yells. "Where are you?"

I exchange amused glances with the man nearby.

She looks around for her friend who is, apparently, nowhere. "Hey," she yells. "I'll just stand up here and do a wild dance!"

The person on the other end says something and she utters a few more choice words. "Baggage claim 10? I'm at 7 or 6 or 8. I don't know." She leans forward and screams, "Where in the — is baggage claim 10? Anybody know?" Nervous people within fifty feet stare at her.

I tell her where to find it. She grabs my hand, stands on her wobbly legs, then presses her hands together like she is praying. "I'm sorry I interrupted you," she slurs. "I hope I didn't bother you."

"No problem."

"It's just that you work and work and work and they pay you a hundred dollars and it isn't enough. I should just ask for more, you know?" She looks at the man nearby and says, "I work hard, but this job just ain't going to cut it."

He looks away.

She surveys the baggage claim again. "Goodbye," she says, "and thank you." She grabs my bag. "Is this mine?"

"No, it's mine."

"Okay, goodbye then."

I pray for that woman as she stumbles down the concourse. But even as I pray, I panic inside. Her eyes and her erratic speech transport me back to five—where adults roll joints and pass them around a circle of haze; where I cower in my bed, hoping no one notices me enough to harass me; where I come face-to-face with people who have lost all sense of control, embracing the erratic dance called drug addiction.

Smelling Mary Jane is an ironic thin place for me, reminding me how fragile life is, how desperate we are to cover up our pain—how close I could've been to embracing her ways, escaping on her wings, becoming a tottering, lost soul who's forgotten social graces.

The grace of God is my Mary Jane. The love of God. It has saved my life. In every way.

3

Snapshot

On my first kindergarten report card, I get a 3 in Cooperation. It should be a 1. My little world has been crumbling around me. Apparently it shows in my behavior in school. But instead of asking why, my mom and stepdad yell at me, tell me to get my act together. I cower away, ashamed.

I am living a nightmare that year, the worst year of my life.

Every single day after kindergarten, I walk to my babysitter's house. Her name is Eva, and she is grouchy. Cigarette smoke encircles her when she walks. She wheezes, complains, and makes her living by babysitting latchkey kids like me. She feeds me, and then waits for two older boys to stop by after school to take me off her hands.

They take me all right. To deep ravines in tangles of sharp sticks and itchy weeds. They pull off my corduroys — the ones my grandmother bought me for kindergarten, then my flowered underwear.

"Don't you want to have kids when you grow up?" one boy says.

"Yes," I whisper. Because I do.

"Well, then, this is what you have to do." They take turns

with me in the forest behind my school. I feel pebbles underneath my legs, cutting, scraping, but I don't move. I run shaking hands over the earth's damp dirt, feeling its grains between my fingers. I cringe when they take sticks and long stalks of grass, using them to violate me again. And again. I clench my five-year-old fists. I count to one hundred. But I don't struggle. I try not to cry. I turn my head to the side, but they force it toward theirs, so I look beyond each boy's face, watching the branches of gigantic evergreens sway gently beneath the gray Northwest sky. Those massive limbs beckon me, and I ache and scream inside to fly into their embrace, but the stones and lichen and bracken hold me captive. I should've known five-year-olds can't fly.

"If you tell anyone," one warns me over and over, like a skipping forty-five, "we'll kill you."

So I keep my mouth firmly shut. Zipped tight. I like life. Death is a ghost that haunts my toss-and-turn dreams, wisping in and through me, dragging me into a dark, empty hole.

The older of the brothers bends even closer, his breath stealing mine. I try to wrench away from his eyes, but he grabs my chin in his strong, angular hands. "Look at me," he spits. "Look at me."

I obey.

"I'm not just talking about you either. Your parents. I'll kill them too." He lets go of my chin, but I still feel his fingerprints there.

"You understand me?"

I nod. I think of my mother's face then—her smooth skin, the way she ties up her hair in a red bandana every day, the way she walks, how she sings loud songs from the record player in the living room, what her laugh sounds like. And though my father Jim no longer lives with us, I believe these boys know who he is and how to find and kill him. I see Jim—his bald head, a camera with a coffee mug—sized lens hanging around his neck, the way he snaps pictures of me like I'm art, and how he hums classical music when he's hiking. I love my mom. I love my dad. I can't be the reason they get snatched by the death ghost.

The boy presses my forehead so the back of my head digs into the dirt, no doubt browning my blonde hair. "Say it," he says.

"I understand you."

"That's my girl."

Sometimes I scream at night. Occasionally it rouses my mom to attend to me, but not always.

We are in the brothers' bedroom, a navy blue sheet draped from the top bunk to the bottom, creating a boy-smelling cave. In the gray light of their shaded bunk, they take more and more of me. The only trees I can watch are in my imagination, so I close my eyes and dream of the Swiss Family Robinson. And even though what the boys do happens too many times to count, it still hurts—angry wasp stings that make going to the bathroom feel like flames. I tell myself to scream. After all, the boys' mom is one room away making cookies for their scout meeting. But my voice flies away, abandoning me like a faraway robin on a branch. So I nurse the wasp stings, walk a little crooked, and don't utter a word about it.

The word they use to describe what they're doing to me is a swear word. A really bad one. It's a word that frequents my step-father's mouth. It punctuates the street language of my neighborhood. I can't bring myself to say it. I'm afraid if I say it out loud, my mouth will be washed out with Joy detergent.

I don't cry.

They laugh.

I don't speak.

They tell dirty jokes.

I lay quietly while they use that word and do that word.

They invite their friends to join in.

Something rises up inside me after others take their turns, something bigger than my fear of death, or my love for my parents. Something called preservation. Or shame. Or maybe my own humanity. I determine that it's over. I have to stop it.

It takes me a very long time to tell my babysitter. Sometimes I get up the gumption only to sputter nonsense and walk away. I can't say that word. Such an ugly, terrible word. I know, too, that once I say the word, everything will change. Those Boy Scouts will get in trouble. Their nice cookie-making mom will be shocked. The babysitter will be fired. My mom and my stepdad will be alarmed. Maybe my mom will tell Jim, my father. There will be crying and anger.

They'll all shout at me. Maybe even blame me.

"I need to tell you something," I say to Eva, clutching a stuffed cat she let me have. She has old toys around her house and the cat is particularly worn out. I take pity on it, love that poor ragged thing. Eva's one act of kindness is giving me that ratty cat.

"What is it?" She inhales a cigarette stub, her eyes blaring impatience.

I tug on her sleeve, pull her ear toward my mouth. "It's a secret," I whisper.

"Well, get on with it then." She blows smoke.

"Those boys? They f—me."

She reels upward, away from my grasp. She seems taller, like her head is nearer to the ceiling than it's ever been. She looms.

I wonder, though. Why is she shocked? What babysitter wouldn't think it peculiar for teenaged boys to take interest in a five-year-old girl every single day? I'm convinced she is not shocked. She's merely been caught in her laziness. Caught like vermin in a trap. So she does the only thing she can do to protect herself. She lies.

"I will tell your mom," she says.

And I believe her.

The next day, the boys come over and take me away. They do the word I whispered to my babysitter. How can this be? How can my mom know about this and let it continue? The evergreens above me no longer bring comfort; they're a menacing twist of dark wood against a too-happy sky, a canopy imprisoning me, holding me captive to that awful word.

I exhale a long, sad breath to the sky, then suck it back in, filling my chest with resolve. No one on earth will take care of me. No one wants to.

I am a nuisance.

Unworthy.

Uncared for.

And no one, not one person, loves me enough to protect me.

Though my voice is silent, my insides say these words: I will protect myself. I'm the only one who can.

I live that little vow the rest of my kindergarten year. I fake sleep. When the boys come around, I am on my babysitter's queen-size bed, eyelids pressed together, my breathing measured and calm. Hearing that familiar knock at the door makes me nearly vomit. I hear Eva open the door to her bedroom. I smell her cigarette. She stands there a good long time, the rasp of her breath catching between drags. "Well, I don't know what to tell you," she says. "But that girl's asleep again. Sorry."

"Wake her up then," one says.

If there's one thing consistent about Eva, it's that she can't be bothered by anyone. That one trait saves me. I picture her waving her hand in the boys' faces, a leave-me-alone in her voice.

The door closes.

I hear the boys' voices as they banter down the alleyway. I open one eye, then both. I have saved myself.

At least for today.

They come back the next day.

I sleep again.

Eva scats them.

I have saved myself.

At least for today.

I would sleep through my entire after-school career had we not moved away that summer. Though it's not easy to understand why God allows boys to do such things to five-year-old me, I can at least see His hand in moving us. I don't see it then, of course, because I don't know a stitch about God. All I know is that those Boy Scouts can't get me when I live thirty miles away.

Recently, I relive that memory of pulling chain-smoking Eva closer. Suddenly the question comes to me:

Why don't I tell my parents first?

If I have guts enough at five to whisper the swear word to the babysitter, why don't I tell the people who have the power to really help me? Eva barely likes me.

My parents are supposed to love me, aren't they? Why don't I say anything? I understand that victims keep secrets, but I tell. I risk my mouth getting washed out with Joy detergent.

But I don't tell my mom because I'm afraid. I don't have to live with Eva the chain-smoking babysitter, but I do have to live with my mom. Forever. Even at five, I know my mom cannot handle my negative emotions. I am not allowed to be sad or angry or upset. If I am, I get in trouble. Big trouble.

So I don't tell her what the brothers do. Because I'm scared. And I don't trust her to take care of me.

For years, I think the babysitter tells my mom — that my mom knows of the abuse and doesn't give a hoot about it.

I bring it up much, much later. A decade later. I am old enough now to know I don't have to use a swear word to describe what happened. And now I know Jesus. He gives me the courage to tell my mom, though I am still deeply afraid.

We are sitting in her hatchback, driving back from my grandparents' house after Sunday dinner. I can feel my heartbeat in my ears. It's time to tell her, I know. But I don't want to. My hands feel slick — a rare thing for someone prone to cold extremities. I swallow. "Mom?"

"Yeah," she answers. So casually.

"When I was five, um ..." I look out the window while fields of horses and cows whir past.

"Yes? What is it?"

"At the babysitter's, I was raped." I spill out the whole story in a staccato rush — the boys, Eva, sleeping, the woods. I hold my breath. I keep the tears in.

"It didn't happen," she says. "You're making it up."

I retell the story, trying to get her to understand. I tell it three or four times while farmland rolls by and my hands turn cold.

Eventually, she believes.

"Eva never told me," she says. I hear a break in her voice, a mother-anguish I can only imagine. She tells me to get counseling, that she'll pay for it, that she's sorry.

As a mom, I panic when I think of my own children, of their vulnerability to people who want to rape their innocence. Even now, I can barely tolerate the thought that my kids might go through the hell I lived. I speak to them about predators. I warn them. I ask them if folks have touched them inappropriately—in places where their swimsuits cover. Even when they answer with satisfactory answers, I still worry. I know how long secrets keep.

How can this memory be a thin place? How can victory possibly come from such a recollection?

Healing makes it a thin place.

Radical, surprising, turn-my-world-upside-down healing.

I am not the violated girl whispering a swear word to chain-smoking Eva.

I am no longer the little girl who feigns sleep.

Or the fifteen-year-old trying to make her mother understand.

I truly am a new creation.

It's taken God thirty-five years to heal me, and He continues to heal me. I am no longer that girl. I'm a woman, loved by God, still struggling with her relationship with her mom, who wants to parent her children well. I am passionate about walking with other girls who had to whisper dirty words, who had to pretend sleep.

Eva's queen-size bed is a strange thin place where I realize the painful truth that humans fail humans, that I will have to take care of myself—which inevitably leads me to realizing I can't. That inadequacy, coupled with my need for a protective, proactive parent leads me right into the embrace of Jesus, who fills up the holes the brothers gave me. And He is still filling those spaces, washing my injuries even today, with life-giving water.

It may seem odd that I experience the presence of Jesus in painful realizations. Like two days ago when I see I was brave enough to tell Eva but not my mom. I'm thankful for His insight because it comes at just the right time. Jesus is a gentleman healer. If He shows me the entire journey of healing before I walk it, I will run the other way, screaming. He shows me a little at a time, thankfully. He lets me chew on it. He meets me in the memory. He shows me again that He's the One who watches over me, protects me. He can handle my negative emotions. They don't surprise Him. He loves me even when I get a 3 in Cooperation, or when I have to whisper a swear word into His ear. Instead of giving lies or criticism, He embraces me. And I'm forever changed because of it.

I see my growth. Today a neighbor stops by with her son, all clad in a Boy Scout uniform. Initially I want to run away. Instead I look at his young, sweet face, listen to him stammer his sales pitch, and tell him yes, I'll buy some popcorn for his fundraiser. Little by little, God heals me — in the most surprising ways.

My father Jim takes a snapshot of me at five. My hair is woefully short. I wear a Peter Pan collared dress that has a polka-dot tie and skirt. Over that is a thrift shop sweater, unbuttoned. Covering the entire ensemble is a fake-wool-lined, gaudy, plaid coat. I'm sitting on his back stoop, holding a passel of roses already opened to the day, petals splayed out in worship. I can't feel their thorns because Jim has put the roses in a dime store vase. An interesting picture, that. But the most difficult part of the picture is my smile. Broad-lipped above a dirty chin, baby teeth still intact. Smiling. Is it taken before the Boy Scouts? Before Eva? Before the 3 in Cooperation? I don't know. But I thank God that at least on the day when Jim snaps pictures, I have a smile to give him.

4

The Crib

I know what those boys do is wrong. That knowledge is a gift, a thinly fragile piece of grace God gives me while my eyes track the creaking trees above me. Most sexual abuse victims take blame; but I don't. The reason I know those boys who raped me were wrong and that I didn't deserve it springs from my short time havened in my grandparents' care. They provided a safe home for me the year before and were the springboard for me to know what was right and wrong.

But sometimes memories are fickle creatures. When relived, what seems tame becomes something altogether different.

Thirty years after I live with my grandparents, a picture comes to mind. It isn't a suppressed memory — I've had it all my life. But a group of folks are praying for me, and asking me to share what comes to mind. I don't. I feel the memory is terribly pedestrian, so ordinary I must be mistaken. Why would God bring that one to the surface?

I share something different. I share the rape story instead — the sensational one.

As prayer continues, I realize I need to revisit my memory, not in a scary New Agey way, but just to see what it is God is trying to say to me. "I am four years old," I say. "And I'm standing in a crib in my grandparents' basement during nap time. But no one will come and get me. From an intercom above my head, my grandmother's echoing voice tells me to lie back down; it's not time to be done with my nap. I stay in my room a good long time. Then I stand again and sing. Eventually she comes downstairs and gets me."

Benign memory.

Except that as I'm prayed for, I connect some dots. Why am I in a crib? Why am I alone? And even more: I realize I'm a burden to my grandparents, that my presence inconveniences them. I am not part of their nearly empty-nested plan.

Later my grandmother tells me this story: "You were so good when you lived at our house. I took you to Bridge with me. You knew you had to be quiet in the other room while we played cards, and you were. Sometimes you came out, but you were always quiet. You liked coming with me to Bridge."

I am sure they did love me, but I learned, then, that to be accepted is to be quiet and convenient. Never making waves. Never disobeying. Never causing my grandparents any extra work.

I am riding my new tricycle down the street, just out of eye-shot of my grandmother. She doesn't chase after me. She is busied somewhere. I continue to the next house with an expansive corner lot. A woman named Boots lives there. She is gardening. She stops and talks to me. Minutes pass. We talk.

My grandmother steps back into the front yard in a flurry — yelling, hollering, beckoning. She spies me around the corner talking to Boots. She scolds me. Rightly so. I have strayed from her boundaries. But why doesn't she notice in the first place?

Memories of my cocooned life replay as folks continue to pray, but it's the crib memory that circles around and crushes my chest.

I can scarcely breathe. I groan in the recollection. The grief presses like a bout of pneumonia turned bad.

For thirty-five years I have believed that in this one point in my life I am wanted, cared for, looked after. Instead I see that I was best kept out of the way — a four-year-old in a crib, with not one memory of my mother during that time.

Prayer continues.

Even my grandparents' home has its flaws, peopled with needy folks who don't always love right. They had lives I interrupted, circles I intruded on, routines I dismantled just by my sheer presence.

I am never really wanted. At least that's how I feel.

The grief.

I stood in that crib, singing to the paneled ceiling, but no one appreciated the melody. It confirms the thought that worms its way through my sojourn here — that I'm unworthy of occupying space on this earth.

The weight of it is now a cannonball on my chest. I cannot roll it off. Those who pray for me watch me struggle. They weep alongside me.

No safe place after all. No haven. No one who really cares just for me.

Of course my mother and grandparents love me, even in that moment when I felt unwanted, illegitimate. My inability to discern their love, coupled with, perhaps, their inability to express it in a way that makes sense to four-year-old me, is what matters. My crib memory is not an indictment of them. In forgiveness, I've had to look myself in the mirror far too many times, realizing I have the same capability to abandon, to be selfish. I'm terribly frail and needy. Sometimes when my children need me, really need me, I walk away — unfeeling. I recall this with compassion for my relatives, for me, for all of us who fail—for all of us who need Jesus' forgiveness.

Eyes closed, lids wet from so much weeping, I see Jesus. He walks into my basement room while the ball of grief still crushes my heart. I see me in the crib, arms stretched to no one, wanting rescue, worth, and significance. Jesus hears my singing. He walks to the crib, pulls down the rail, and lifts me to Himself. He holds me. Whispers blessings over me. Tells me He is my safe place, my conscience, my Daddy who won't leave. My breathing slows. In one heaving yawp, the ball lumbers off my chest. I am like Joshua when the Lord told him, " 'Today I have rolled away the reproach of Egypt from you.' So the name of that place is called Gilgal to this day" (Joshua 5:9 NASB).

The cool thing: Gilgal sounds like the Hebrew word *roll*. In that holy, crushing thin place, in the ethereal place of gauzy memory, God rolls the reproach of my childhood from me. Jesus comes near, so near I can nearly feel His embrace. He enters into the place I once thought my haven, shows me its flaws. He becomes my refuge—the only One who truly can be.

Though I'm raw recollecting the memory, peace holds my hand. I may not have had a safe place back then. I may have been annoyingly in the way. But to God I am precious, never a burden, always delighted in. Standing in the crib, anticipating His embrace, I rest there today.

At times I get stuck in that crib, wallowing in my rightness to be angry. I wear the word victim like a badge of honor—my own purple heart. I see what others do more than I see what I'm capable of. I hate to admit how many times my heart's been bitter and cold—a result of nurturing my wounds instead of letting God heal them. I linger over Mary in the crib and forget about Jesus lifting me from that crib.

The memory is a thin place where I have the painful privilege of extending forgiveness again, to walk with Jesus through the memory with grace-filled eyes. Any time I'm wronged (or, in this case, perceive I am wronged), I have a window to see Jesus clearer by the way I react. If I forgive, I get to experience Him. If I growl bitterness, He seems farther away. Forgiving is the deepest kinship I've experienced with Jesus so far, but it's not an easy kinship:

When I suffer
For something I didn't do
When I pay the price
For someone else's sin
I rant and stomp my feet
And mutter one thousand
Renditions of
It's not fair

But You kept silent
As a mouse
Contented
Never ranting,
Weeping
Drops of blood
For the cross
You had to bear

On my behalf

I rant today
Because You didn't,
Because Your sacred shoulders
Willingly bore my shame
In silence

I understand a mouse-sized bit
Your quiet sacrifice
As I wear the sin of another
Unwillingly
Like a scratchy coat
In summer's heat

All those words I've heard
About walking in Your footfalls
Are true
But it isn't easy
Wearing this coat
For so long

Maybe we can be kin
In this mouse-muttering
Sacrifice
As the sweat beats down
On earthen brow
And sacred

And maybe through
The scratch of another's sin
I can finally understand
Your outrageous gift
And love You
All the more

In silence

Age grants me a surprising blessing: I understand true life doesn't happen when I constantly gaze backwards, mulling over all the injustices others have done or I have done to others. Life is a tiptoeing anticipating of the future. Oswald Chambers says it well: "Let the past sleep, but let it sleep on the bosom of Christ, and go out into the irresistible future with him."[2] I see now that life is not simply a pensive look back to the known, but a daring leap forward to the unknown. Forgiveness bridges the crib memory and living abundantly today.

In my journal I scrawl words from Mark Buchanan. He captures so well this stew of memory and forgiveness and longing to live life well. "Her past was a tragedy to lament," he writes, "but her future was an epic to anticipate ... which is a simple way to say: what *will* happen matters more than what *has* happened."[3]

I am guilty of many things in my life, but it never occurs to me that perhaps the greatest regret I have is staying stuck in bully memories. Today I am no longer standing in the crib. I am in Jesus' arms, joyfully anticipating the future.

5

Envy

At five, envy woos me.

Janine, with her perfect blonde Cindy Brady hair and her child-sized kitchen, has everything I want. The refrigerator, as tall as she is, boasts side-by-side doors — something even my family's fridge doesn't have. Our fridge is a roundish monster from the 50s, the kind where the freezer compartment is revealed by opening the ponderous fridge door. My mom seldom defrosts the poor freezer, so all we can fit in there is one pathetic ice cube tray.

But Janine — she has it all. A side-by-side pretend fridge with a fake icemaker in the door. Little plastic cubes plop out on command. Her grandmother stocks her fridge (and pantry, and oven, and sink) with fake food, stuffing pieces of cut-to-fit Styrofoam into cereal boxes, Jiffy muffin mixes, Hamburger Helper. But the pièce de résistance is the real eggs. Grandma saves an egg carton, cracks the eggs from its belly, and then washes one half of each shell. When she put the eggshell tops back into the carton, they look just like real eggs (maybe because they are). If I knew about salmonella then, I'd have wished it upon perfect Janine with her Betty Crocker kitchen.

The envy doesn't go away when I'm grown. I pine for my

daughters to have a fancy-schmancy kitchen like Janine, but we don't have the money to buy the beautiful plastic kitchens of the new generation. We settle for a handmade one, passed on to us by friends whose children have enjoyed it for several years. I spend time refinishing the kitchen, making it just so. My girls enjoy it, but they don't relish it the way I would have.

It occurs to me that my longing for Janine's plastic kitchen is really a longing for her grandmother — a woman who lavishes love, affection, and sterilized eggshells on her granddaughter. Her grandmother's generosity sparks my longing for a whimsical, sacrificial love. Janine's grandmother has no idea, I'm sure, that her kindness helps me glimpse the lavish kindness of God.

It gladdens me to no end that, perhaps, my children understand this affection from broken me. That they see, through the tangibility of a kitchen made with love, I love them, and that God loves them as well. My friend Renee tells me, "I can see you love your children by the way you decorate their rooms." She probably doesn't know she is speaking redemption over me, showing that God has dared to enter my life and remake me — like a hotel maid makes an unmade bed — to be the mom I always longed for.

The only way to turn around envy is to offer gratitude for what you have — to give thanks for what *God* has done in you and for you. My friend Hud says gratitude is perhaps the greatest indicator of where we are with Jesus. The more gratitude, the closer we are to the whispers of Jesus.

I don't grow up with gratitude firmly rooted in my heart. I'd love to be able to say that after pining for all things Janine, I become free of envying others. I wish for the wisdom of Solomon: "And I saw that all labor and all achievement spring from man's envy of his neighbor. This too is meaningless, a chasing after the wind" (Ecclesiastes 4:4). I'm afraid to read that verse again. If I really take it to heart, I'll see how much of my achieving is based on envy.

In the springtime of childhood, I make quiet, envious vows.

I meet Pam, whose stay-at-home mom makes egg salad sandwiches, Christmas caroling dolls out of old Reader's Digests, and all her polyester pantsuits. I seethe and long for things to be different in my life. I vow I'll be a stay-at-home mom, that I'll make things with my hands, that I'll sew clothes for my children. (Thank goodness I don't do the latter; I doubt my children would appreciate matching polyester pantsuits.)

Pam, along with all her other cohorts in first grade, carries lunch in a beautiful lunch pail; I bring a ratty old lunch bag. She has Cheetos tucked away in the most amazing plastic food bags; I have crackers wrapped in waxed paper. Kids don't tease me for my bagged lunches full of wax-wrapped food, but something inside me despises my humble fare. How I long for a Hostess Ho-Ho or a peanut butter and jelly sandwich tucked inside a baggie. I envy my classmates' lives, so I hide my lunches under my bed and starve. No wonder I am thin! Better to save face than to bring a lunch like that every day. This works well for me, in spite of my hunger, until my mom discovers the moldy stash beneath my bed.

"You'll have to make your own lunches from now on," she says.

I cringe. My face burns.

"Do you know how long it takes me to make your lunches — and you throw them away? Do you realize how that makes me feel?"

The envy bug bites again and again. Someone always has a better home, nicer family, trendier clothes.

I am guilty of envying unreality too. In my need for a nuclear family, I dream of living inside the split-level Brady Bunch home.

I'll be beautiful Marsha, a matriarch of sorts over the rest of my five siblings. Smiling Alice will make lunches for me, complete with American cheese sandwiches. I'll have the right clothes, the right neighborhood, the right social status. I'll have it all.

But life is not the Brady Bunch.

We move again when I start sixth grade—a painful move since I leave behind my very best friend in the whole wide world. She shouldered my grief over losing Jim. She cried with me when my stepfather and mother didn't know what to do with my tears. And now I forsake the security of a three-year friendship in lieu of befriending strangers.

On the first day of sixth grade, bully girls pull me to the edge of the outdoor track and scowl words into my soul. "Do you have San Francisco Riding Gear?" they ask.

One girl with blonde frizzy hair and a sneer turns around, lifts her shirt slightly, and proudly declares, "These jeans are San Francisco Riding Gear. If you want to be popular, you have to buy them." The bottoms of the jeans cover the length of her feet and drag along the muddy ground. I have never seen such wide denim in my life—like elephant legs, only blue with orange triple stitching down the side.

I have no idea what she is talking about. I look down at my pathetically thin-legged Sears Roebuck jeans. They are—gasp!—red. I want to die. Though I don't even like the way the other girl's jeans look, I know I have to have some to fit in with this crowd, a passel of girls who frighten me. I start bothering my mother about this. Problem is, Dumbo-legged jeans are expensive. One pair costs over thirty dollars and only one store in town carries them. I suffer through my shameful Sears Toughskins for six months, cementing my nerd-dom in the eyes of all cool kids.

Then one magical day in February, my birthday to be exact,

my mom splurges and purchases three pairs of denim coolness. And some silky tops, also all the rage. I strut into my elementary school the next day, smile wider than the bottoms of my San Francisco Riding Gear.

You'll think that as I'm telling you this cautionary tale of envy, I'll say things never change, that all that envy and pining mean nothing. But the truth is, everything changes.

In one blessed twenty-four hour period, I morph from nerd extraordinaire to with-it girl. Derek asks me to "go with him." I immediately fit in with the right crowd—all because of three pairs of jeans.

I realize envy works. I want something and I think it will satisfy, so I do all sorts of acrobatics to get it. And for a while everything's right with the world.

Then I want more.

And more.

And more.

Of course, no amount of wide-legged jeans could fill my aching emptiness. The day-after-my-birthday is a thin place where I understand clearly that stuff can't fill me. But I keep on the treadmill, running after clothing, makeup, music—anything that will help me be loved by the cool crowd.

Two things turn my heart away from envy. One is the pain others have inflicted on me because of it. The other is the pain inflicted on Jesus because of it.

In college, I receive a four-page, single-spaced typed letter from a good friend. "I need to give you this," she says, her voice a mixture of nervousness and melancholy. "Out of obedience." She leaves me alone in my dorm room with the simple white-paged letter. I unfold it, smoothing the pages. I am unsettled by her grave tone because we share a mutually happy friendship. We pray for revival on the campus. We talk about boys and our penchant for crushes. We eat breakfasts, lunches, and dinners together. We worship Jesus flat out—both in raucous, charismatic songs, hands thrust to the ceiling, begging God to come down and fill us. We pray for each other's emotional healing. We keep each other's secrets.

I see the words, but I hardly believe them—words like, "I have not liked you for a long time" and "You're pretty and smart and can sing and it makes me angry because I am none of those things." She recounts all the reasons she is envious of me. And then she apologizes, asking my forgiveness for her bitterness.

Our conversation in the letter's aftermath is stilted. How do you respond to something like that? Should I apologize for who I am? Tell her I'm sorry she feels that way? I forgive her, tell her how brave she is for admitting such things, and ask her if I've done anything specifically to hurt her. Our friendship doesn't end. We work it out. But the working out isn't easy.

Being on the other end of that kind of envy helps me realize that envy is not trivial. Job 5:2 says, "Envy slays the simple." It kills me. It kills others. It decays my soul. "A heart at peace gives life to the body, but envy rots the bones" (Proverbs 14:30). When I camp in the New Testament, I am stunned to see envy saddled alongside some pretty hefty sins: greed, malice, deceit, lewdness, slander, arrogance, folly, wickedness, evil, depravity, murder, strife, drunkenness, orgies, foolishness, disobedience, hatefulness, selfish ambition. Yet I treat envy as if it were a puppy needing to be potty trained—harmless and slightly entertaining.

It's somewhat easy to spout off the pain others inflict, but it's another thing altogether to admit my own envies. I envy people made in the image of God, cutting them down in my head with words too embarrassing to write. I am petty. Mean. I lack grace.

It hurts me when I realize envy is what kills Jesus — nails His sacred hands and feet to the cross. Speaking of Pilate and the Pharisees, Matthew says, "For he knew it was out of envy that they had handed Jesus over to him" (Matthew 27:18). Jesus does things the Pharisees can't do. Raises the dead. Heals people. Bucks convention for the sake of His Father's glory. Jesus possesses qualities the Pharisees will never have, like authority, presence, and popularity. The envious elite seethe that so many folks leave everything behind to follow this Man. The mass exodus threatens their ministries. So to preserve the status quo, but more likely to keep face, they deliver Jesus to be crucified. They mask it all in piety.

I fear I do the same.

6

Pickets

I stare at the computer screen. It's a picture of a small white house, set back from the road. It preens in cottage glory. A perennial garden winks at me, but I don't smile. Surrounding the home in the picture is a white picket fence — my dream. My friends know this dream. My kids know it. My husband builds me one because he knows my penchant for pickets.

But this house, all prettied up, is not the house of my dreams.

I am five when I live in this house. I set up a little oasis in a tiny appendage to the house (where our water meter lives) — a tiny boxed-off place where I stow treasures. I make my Easter candy go a long way in there, protected by plastic eggs and the fact that no one sees. It's one of the many secrets I keep in that house.

In the alleyway is the cane-shaking neighbor, a Seattle version of Mrs. Dubose in *To Kill a Mockingbird* who hollers at Scout and Jem. Only my neighbor yells death at me when I eat the blackberries spilling over her fence.

"You'll die. They're poison," she screams.

I fling myself on my bed, tortured at the thought that in a few minutes I will die. I don't die, but part of me wishes I did.

I have two friends while I live in that little white home: one real, one imaginary. I meet Kimi (real) when my mom tells me to go out and find a friend. She must feel weary bearing the weight of being my only companion, and in exasperation sends me hunting.

I turn left out of my picketed gate, take another left, pass my alleyway, then see a little girl playing in a glassed-in porch. I knock on the door and ask the girl's mom if she can play with me. That's how Kimi and I meet. I'm not sure how I meet DeeDee (imaginary). She turns up around the same time the neighborhood boys do. I tell her things no one else hears or knows. She keeps the secrets of the little white house and doesn't tell a soul.

Spying the house thirty-five years later, fixed up with fresh paint and a white picket fence, curdles my stomach. The secrets it holds belie its charming exterior. I delete the image, asking the sender to please not email me another picture of that house. But the image stays seared in my memory nonetheless, as stark as bare branches against the bluest sky.

We move to a new house—dark brown with pink trim. It's off the main road down a gravel drive. Woods live to the left of the house where I play with a neighbor girl. I have no little spot to call my own, no little cubby adjoining the house. All I have is my room. I learn to ride my first bike down the gravelly road. And I learn that a home is never really safe.

Standing on the front porch, I smell something strange.

"It smells like a swimming pool," I say.

My mom's boyfriend tries to unlock the front door, only to find it gives too easily.

Ketchup splatters the living room walls. Bleach emanates from the heat register vents. Every cabinet is opened. Food litters the kitchen floor. A candle is broken, my mother's jewelry picked through. Whoever vandalized the house stole things that don't work. My mom and her boyfriend joke at the inability of the crooks to take the right things. But I don't laugh. I cower and cry. I pull the covers over my head and shake, knowing the Boogie Man will soon come to get me.

I know, because of the ghosts.

"See here," someone says after pulling up our living room rug, revealing a kidney-shaped dark purple stain the size of me. "Some poor soul died here. That's his blood."

Others tell me that ghosts make the racket I hear at night — the slamming of cabinets past midnight. "And if you listen real careful, you can hear a dead granny rocking her chair in the attic, right above your bed."

Ralph knows this too and is fascinated by it all. He tries to find the ghosts, and he swears he hears them. Ralph is the son of my mom's friend. Pudgy, dirty, and a little older, he spends the night whenever his mom comes over to party. Ralph shares my twin bed. He kicks me. He smells like sour milk and sweat. He flails and hogs the bed. He rolls over onto me while I hug the wall. I elbow him away.

Sometimes we giggle. I know it sounds strange that an eight- or nine-year-old boy giggles, but you don't know Ralph. He giggles. And jumps on my bed. He corrals me into jumping too, making helter-skelter racket. After several warnings, my stepdad (my mom's marriage number three) yells at us for our frivolity.

We relocate again, trading the brown and pink house for a bigger house that was once white, now grayed with peeling paint. It's beauty to my mom, with its acreage for our horses.

This is the home I run to after my father's funeral. I run upstairs to my attic room, pull the covers over my head, and wail —but quietly. I scream grief into my Donny Osmond pillowcase. Although he smiles back at me, he is no comfort.

Sometimes my grief leaks out. Though I keep quiet for several months after Jim's death, sadness spills out of my mouth from my room upstairs. I need to know someone hears my cries. I'm tired of trying to cope with Jim's death alone. I hear the thwap of my mom's riding boots on the steep wooden stairs leading to my room. My eyes are wet and itchy from crying.

"What are you doing?" she asks.

"I'm sad about Jim dying," I say. I wait for her hug, for the feeling of her hand against my head, the way she smoothes away the hair from my face.

"It's time to be over that now." She doesn't stoop to touch me. Her voice is far away, pinched, distracted.

I feel like a drama queen, a girl who overreacts to grief.

Her footsteps sound louder as they clonk down the stairs, leaving me with tears spent in vain, and a pillow with which I now muffle my cries.

The grief breaks out anyway. I am alone, mucking out the horse stalls. Clods of urine-heavy cedar shavings cling to my pitchfork. Horse manure, once green, now rolls off the tines—brown balls of excrement hard as dried earth. I don't swear, but I yell every time I dig the tines into the packed stall bed. This horse stall is my life—dirty, neglected, overwhelming. And I am left alone to try to tidy it. Wheelbarrow full after wheelbarrow full, yet the stall never loses its horse smell, never really looks clean.

More shoveling.

I start crying. Since no one is around, I holler my life to the batten-board ceiling, weeping my helplessness in the face of the impossible task.

"I can't do this. I can't. I can't."

Another wheelbarrow dumped into the pasture adjoining the stall.

"I'll never finish. It's not fair."

On and on I yell about everything—stalls, horses, Jim.

I hear a voice.

I reel around.

It's Tom, the hired boy, not much older than me.

"Are you okay?"

I know my face is red, part from exertion, part from embarrassment. How much did he hear? Did he catch all my rants?

He walks toward me, looks like he's concerned. He opens the stall door, comes inside. He stands nearly rubber boot to rubber boot with me.

I step back.

He wants to comfort fifth grade me with his seventh grade self.

"I need to go inside," I lie. I hand him the pitchfork and scurry out.

Right before sixth grade we settle ourselves into a metal-sided farmhouse, this one with ten acres and a creek, two outbuildings, and a barn. I spend more time in that house than my mom or her third husband do. I beat them both home from work, take care of the horses, dog, and cats, and start my journey toward becoming a great cook at thirteen, making my own dinners. The house echoes. I talk to my cats and dog. I call my friends. Television families, bless their black and white hearts, become my sisters and brothers and mothers and fathers. Without them, the farmhouse seems awfully, painfully silent.

And when my mom and stepdad divorce, it gets even quieter.

When Jesus woos me as a freshman in high school, and I meet Him at Young Life camp the next year, I am suddenly aware I am no longer alone. All the junior-high suicidal thoughts smother in His embrace. I am full. I am different. I share the company of God. On the wings of that joy, I sit down with my mom to tell her the Good News.

"I met Jesus!"

"What?"

"Jesus!" I tell her all about the camp, about salvation, about heaven and hell, death and resurrection. I am a walking evangelist, thrilled at the opportunity to help my mom be happy.

"How do you know Young Life's not a cult?" she asks.

I sit back, noting the anger behind her words. "What?"

"A cult. How do you know they haven't brainwashed you?"

I have nothing to say other than, "I met Jesus," hoping that would be enough.

But it's not.

"Mom." I am crying now. "Don't you want to go to heaven?"

"When I die, I'm dead. That's the end of me." She looks away.

I try to share some more, but her visible anger clogs my words like tangled hair in a drain.

She stands and walks out of the living room.

I am more alone than ever.

The little white cottage, the brown and pink home, the house with peeling paint, the farmhouse—none truly protect me. They loom as ruffian memories, reminding me of what I seldom discover as a child—a feeling of home, a connected family, a place of joy instead of isolation.

I long for a home that represents something different. A green blanket of grass, glistening after rain — my children imprinting footprints on the lawn, marking their happy territory. Laughter. A mom and a dad who love each other. A sanctuary of unconditional love where children thrive and sing and rest and experience over-the-top comfort. A haven enclosed by fictitious pickets.

It comes one night, that home.

I am sitting with Sophie, Aidan, Julia, and Patrick around our table. We are eating dinner and sharing our days. I battle inside myself, wondering if I should share my frustrating day or just let it rest securely inside my head. Such heaviness settles on me that I don't want to infect my children. But when it's my turn, I make a snap decision to speak up.

"I've had a hard day," I tell them. "I got another book rejection." I expand the story, letting my family know the wrenching details. I take in a deep breath. "And here's the thing. When I'm rejected, it sends me to this very dark pit, to this place where I wonder if I'm worthy enough to take up space on this earth." I point my finger into the table. "This space right here."

"Mommy," Julia says. "I love you. I'm so glad God made you to be my mommy."

"I don't know where I'd be without you," Sophie says.

"Please don't feel like that," Aidan tells me.

"I love you." Patrick grabs my hand.

In that embrace of words, I am home.

My mind flips between disparate images — the picket-encircled white cottage belying the torment of memories locked inside its gate, and the faces of my family declaring their love for me. I linger on the pickets one last time, then turn full-faced to my family. People who want me. Who cherish me. Whose love protects and heals me. Theirs is the image that grows more colorfully vibrant, while the other fades to black and white.

7

Write Away

"I want you to give your mother this," my second grade teacher says. She gives me a handwritten note. I can see her perfect penmanship through the white paper. Will I be in trouble again? Why would my teacher give me a note?

I palm the note in my coat pocket on my way to daycare. It sits next to my stomach, burning a hole through the thin lining of my jacket. What does it say?

I toy with throwing it away, letting the garbage can's wide mouth eat it for good, but my conscience won't let me. It would be wrong. And besides, the teacher would ask whether I gave it to my mom or not. I couldn't lie.

When my mom picks me up from daycare, I do not tell her about the note. As she unlocks the front door, I feel the note, fingering it, wondering what it will mean. I pull it out of my pocket and hand it to my mom. My hand is trembling.

"What is this?" she asks.

"I don't know," I say. "My teacher wants you to have it."

She sits at the kitchen table. I stand. She unfolds the note. Behind her round John Lennon glasses, I watch her eyes scan the letter. She has no reaction—no anger, no happiness. But a smile plays on her lips when she finishes. She hands the note to me.

My second grade teacher writes how I have a gift for words. That my mind is terribly creative. That I should be a writer. I let out a breath, thankful I won't be punished. My teacher's words play in my head like a favorite song, never over-listened-to. I am a writer. A writer.

So I scribble my life onto the page. My diary becomes the place I grapple with my questions and difficulties. It's the place I record my tears and replay the conversations that perplex me. When someone tells me, "I didn't say that," my diary becomes the place where I check my sanity, and find out that the person did say that because it's written down for all posterity. Over the years, these notebooks become the place I lament. I expect. I list. I observe. I pray. I wrestle.

In a very real way, I write away my pain.

In college, I write my first short story, and when I read it out loud to friends, I know. This is the thing God wants me to do. I feel it way down deep. After all, my father was a writer — an essayist and poet, an Assistant Professor of English. His literary genius, I hope, rubs off on me. His love of the English language flows through my veins, though in that realization, I worry. I read what he writes at the beginning of his writing journey — poetry of sweetness and light, prayers to God — and I can't reconcile it with what he writes later — dark, empty words grasping at nothing. My father dies tortured, one of those geniuses too smart for the world. If I delve into writing, will I give in to madness? Will my words tangle my sanity?

But God proves otherwise, bless Him. If anything, my words on a page have led to tremendous amounts of healing, often in surprising ways. When I write *Building the Christian Family You Never Had*, I am nearly debilitated as I fashion the chapters. I worry how the book will affect my family of origin. I fret over every single word. I nearly give up. But God keeps me at it. And when it's released to the wind (and Barnes and Noble!), I feel paradoxical freedom. Writing that book helps me grow up, to be an adult, to say what needs to be said. I trust God in an entirely new way, though the path toward that trust is painful.

I write that book to help other pioneer parents who don't want to duplicate the homes they are raised in; but in the writing, God helps me. He digs me out of a deep pit, sets my feet on a rock, and gives me freedom.

When I write *Watching the Tree Limbs*, I have no idea how God will use that book in my own life. It's the story of a girl, nine years old, who is raped by a neighborhood bully. It's a mystery about a girl searching for her parents. I'm sure you see the similarities. I've read enough to know that a person's first novel is nearly always autobiographical. Imagine my surprise when my editor writes that terribly long revision letter—oh the pain!—and tells me something utterly surprising: my protagonist has no emotional responses to the horrible things that happen in her life. I look through the manuscript, trying to prove my editor wrong, but I cannot. All at once I see that I've made my character act the way I am expected to act in my home growing up. Because I am not allowed to have negative emotions as a child, I put the same restrictions on my character.

In one of the most cathartic writing experiences of my life, I walk through my manuscript, giving my character the emotions I am not allowed to have. I grieve my childhood; but in so doing, I am set free. Writing that book is a thin place where I see God's desire to heal me, and I understand that He loves me no matter what emotions I express. It opens my eyes to my sometimes-flawed parenting. I clearly see how I squelch my kids' negative emotions, and, by God's grace, I learn to embrace my kids no matter how they're feeling.

All that from writing a book.

I could say my writing is all for me, and it'd be a hint of truth. So much of what I write is cathartic. But I'm also reminded how God heaps blessings on me like a second helping of mashed potatoes. Spoonful by spoonful, He shows me that my paltry words touch others. A woman shares her rape for the first time and starts the journey of healing. A pioneer parent feels understood. A mom struggling with her kids runs to Jesus for strength. It's almost too much — to be given a gift that helps me and blesses others. Oh, the boundless, surprising grace of Jesus!

I have this little idea that worms its way through my head, that perhaps God is redeeming my father's writing through my pen. He's completing my father's genius in me, but He's doing it through my own frailty. I'm no genius. I'm a mess half the time. But God's great work of redemption spans the generations. When I put words to the page, I wonder if my dad can see me. Does he smile? When I see pieces of his handwriting, how achingly similar his penmanship is to mine, I wonder. And then I look at my daughter Sophie who published her first article at fourteen years old. Perhaps the gift God gave my father spills over into my prose, touching Sophie's pen.

All I can say is: let the healing begin.

8

Like Me

At ten years old, I am used to standing in the wings, used to being overlooked. Other than my best friend with whom I've forged a comfortable, albeit slightly obsessive bond, I learn to orchestrate life alone.

It's the same as I stand outside my horse's stall at the county fair. I've won first and second place (which really doesn't mean much — everyone does). My horse stands bored, kicking at the straw under her hooves. A group of girls from my 4-H club walk over to me. They're older, much older, in their teens. Shari looks at me, eyeing my Toughskins jeans, my printed T-shirt.

"You wanna come with us?" She looks at the group who feign a half interest in her proposition. "We're riding every single ride in the fair, kind of like a challenge. You game?"

Am I!

I nod.

I follow them, smiling. Their plan? To start at the kiddie rides — those motorcycles that go round and round or the slide you go down in a burlap sack — eventually graduating to the bigger rides until they've ridden every single ride in the fair.

But I have to go to the restroom.

They walk fast, gabbing like teenaged horse girls do—about boys, horses, boys, cotton candy, and makeup. It's a world I want to belong to. I realize that telling these girls that I have to go to the bathroom is akin to social suicide, so I keep my mouth shut and hope my bladder will cooperate.

We've ridden every silly small ride and now I know I must find a restroom. Taking a deep breath, I approach Shari. "Um, I need to go the bathroom."

She rolls her eyes, just as I expect her to. "Oh, come on. We're not done yet. Let's go on the Zipper, okay? Then you can go."

I agree. We scream our way through the Zipper. Halfway through I feel twin urges: to pee and throw up. But everything stays put, thankfully.

I am ready to run like a wild horse to the port-a-potties nearby when Shari stops me. "Oh, come on. We only have one ride left. After we're finished with the Scrambler, you can go to the restroom."

My eyes feel like they're crossing. I know I should walk away. But the lure of acceptance by Shari and her friends is stronger than my need to relieve. I coddle my self-will and head to the Scrambler.

I sit next to Shari and her friend, we three sandwiched together as the ride starts. I concentrate on not wetting my pants. For a while I feel like I've mastered myself ... until my seatmates start laughing. I try not to smile. I beg myself not to laugh. I try to focus on something, anything, but the whir of the ride and the way it scrambles everything I see prevents me from focusing.

I laugh.

And then I pee.

Bladder relief and social terror overwhelm me. In that moment, I am thankful for three things:

One, that it's only me who is wet.

Two, the ride isn't that fast, so my urine is puddled on my side of the car.

Three, we're almost done.

In the worst two seconds of my life, the Carnie casts a sickly gaze our way and flips the Scrambler's "go fast" switch. All at once, the pee I've safely kept on my side of the car seeps beneath me to reach my friends' rear ends. The girls scream, each looking at me wild-eyed. The ride stops.

"Gross!" Shari's friend yells.

"What have you done? I can't believe you peed on me," Shari says. The cool girls can't get away from me fast enough. They run away, laughing, mocking, jeering. I'm left alone — only a wet backside to keep me company, the stench following me as I work my way through the maze of fair rides to find a place to hide.

I want people to like me. I do all sorts of contortions to make it so — not so dramatic as shunning the port-a-potty when nature calls, but probably more soul damaging. I conform myself to others' expectations. I become a chameleon, melding into the likes and dislikes of my friends. It's been an obsession, this insatiable need to be liked; and because it's so strong, I get hurt — a lot, and unnecessarily.

At five years old and forty, my stomach rocks and rolls inside me. I ache.

At five, my "friends" steal my tricycle. One day my prized purple tricycle sits happily in my backyard. The next day it's gone. A week later, I see a neighbor kid with my tricycle, one foot on the back bumper, the other pushing the trike down the alleyway. He's far too big for it.

"That's mine," I tell him.

He points to the handlebars. They've been turned upside down. "No, it's not. Yours didn't look like this."

I look around. No one is around to help me. Alone in the alley, I say it again. "It's mine."

"Yours had tassels. This one ain't got any. See?" He points to the rubber handles where my tassels once hung. They'd been ripped out.

He speeds away, laughing. He'd been my friend.

I sell lemonade where my yard meets the sidewalk. Though my mom warns me not to take my silver dollars to the curb, I insist. I want people to see that I have change. I want my friends to understand I'm not poor. I sell my lemonade, and lose those silver dollars—not so mysteriously.

At forty, I have a bike; it's not purple, it has no tassels, but it's mine. I've got some money to rub together; not silver dollars, but a few green ones. Friends don't try to take things like that today. The things friends take now are far more excruciating. One gossips, saying things that aren't true. Another scorns. It doesn't feel much different, seeing my tricycle or reputation rearranged. I've befriended bullies, thirty-five years apart.

Trust is a precious thing. And I give it away far too often. Like laundry hanging on a line, skivvies flying on an erratic breeze, I air myself for others to see and soil. I don't exactly know where I should position myself—is there such a thing as too much trust? Too little? How long do I give? Isn't Jesus' love unending? Shouldn't I love everyone, even when turning the other cheek gives me whiplash? Or when my tricycle rolls away under the sneakered feet of former friends?

I tether myself to people who wish upon me illness, or acne, or failure. I chase after people who don't like me, trying to convince them they're wrong. I've made as my god the wavering opinions of others. No wonder I scamper after each one, begging. "Like me, please. I'm not as bad as you think."

Why can't I be okay when someone is mad at me? Why can't I call a bully a bully and walk away? Why do I cling to those who hurt me the most, suffering years in the hope of catching a hint of approval?

Ridiculous truth incoming: I'm insecure at heart.

I love to order my world. When others don't like me, my world breaks apart. And I panic. I can be secure when everyone approves.

During my eighth grade year, a tower of a girl, taller than the biggest boys—even the football players—decides she doesn't like me. Andrea writes notes to friends, spelling out my demise. She follows me down hallways. She claws her way into my dreams.

"Andrea's gonna get you," her friend tells me.

I hold my stomach and wish for death. Anything is better than anticipating Andrea.

She follows me to an area behind the softball fields. She stands, angry hands on angry hips, but she doesn't hit me. She lets me off the hook, but only when I promise not to like the boy she's "in love with." I'm a bargainer, even then.

The pathetic truth is that even today I feel stuck in eighth grade. I cower to other Andreas like a beaten puppy that recoils beneath a raised hand. I believe God wants to grind this out of me, like heavenly Roto-Rooter. He's been at me about this for three years, and still I chase Andrea.

I drive myself nutty, all for the sake of wanting every single person on this earth to like me. Notice me. Not criticize me.

Lying in bed, I lament to my husband that I don't deal well with criticism. It's not that I can't physically hear it; it's that I hear it with a megaphone to my ear. I have a secret little recording device that digitally records the criticism (at the same screeching volume) and plays it over and over in my head, adding embellishments for good measure — tidbits like, "You're no good. You failed your friend. You'll never get it right."

Someone tells me this week that I need to learn how to be gentler on myself. Which, of course, I take as criticism. And replay, ad nauseum, to my husband. "What do you think she meant? Why aren't I gentle on myself?"

I ask him to think on it, pray about it, and get back to me.

But he comes back to me, baffled.

Why indeed?

Is it that I'm a megalomaniac, only happy when I'm perfect at everything? If that is the case, then I don't need Jesus, do I?

If I distill it down, I think it has to do with inferiority. When I hear someone wants to meet me because I am "famous," I nearly choke on my smoothie. Me? Ha!

I could give the holy reason why I feel inferior to others: "Because that's how Jesus would like it — me lowly, Him exalted." But I think something more insidious is at work here. I think I *need* to be everything to everybody. I panic when I let someone down. I panic when I disappoint a friend. Why? Because I'm afraid.

I'm afraid folks won't love me if they see my shortcomings. It's a strange dichotomy. I fancy myself authentic, unafraid to share my warts; but if I directly disappoint someone, I want to crawl in a hole. Even though I know it's a lie, I tend to believe that in order to be valued and loved, I must never do anything to hurt anyone. Likewise, in order to love myself, I must never do anything wrong.

That sure doesn't leave room for grace, does it?

Why does everything spin down to this: my titanic struggle with God's love for me? He loves me, this I know. And yet I struggle. Because I don't measure up. My mind says yes, but my heart says, "He will love me ONLY IF I . . ."

Criticism confirms that I blow it all the time, that I'm not worthy to take up space on this earth. I cherish the criticism, though I don't know why. Call me masochistic, I suppose. I hold insults in my hands like truffles begging to be savored. But when I open my hand, all I see is a chocolaty mess. And then I realize they aren't truffles at all, but brown sticky mud, the kind we have in our Texas yard. Why do I hold on instead of letting go and allowing Jesus to wash my hands?

Maybe it's that I love to make mud pies from the insults of others.

It doesn't make sense!

But I still do it.

A friend gives me Psalm 73. I muddy my Bible's pages as I read it.

> When my heart was embittered and I was pierced within, then I was senseless and ignorant; I was like a beast before You. Nevertheless I am continually with You; You have taken hold of my right hand. With Your counsel You will guide me, and afterward receive me to glory. Whom have I in heaven but You? And besides You, I desire nothing on earth. My flesh and my heart may fail, but God is the strength of my heart and my portion forever. For, behold, those who are far from You will perish; You have destroyed all those who are unfaithful to You. But as for me, the nearness of God is my good; I have made the Lord God my refuge, that I may tell of all Your works.
>
> Psalm 73:21–28 NASB

I break into prayer after consuming the Psalm: Oh, dear Lord, take the mud of others' disdain. Wash my hands. Make me clean. Take away my embittered heart. I want to say, "Besides You, I desire nothing on this earth"; but to be honest, my very core still desires for everyone to like me. Oh, strip me of that need for others' approval. Help me to long for only Yours. Help, Jesus. I know You understand. Help me to lean into Your arms when my hands are dirtied with other people's words. Help me to offer them to You and You alone. Like prayer. Or worship. Amen.

Selah.

It all comes down to who you want to like you. For so long, far too long, I've wanted the whole wide world to like me, to applaud me. If the whole wide world (the selfsame world God holds in His hands) likes me, then I will be okay. Which will work, if this is true. But it's not. I slam into verses like, "For am I now seeking the favor of men, or of God? Or am I striving to please men? If I were still trying to please men, I would not be a bond-servant of Christ" (Galatians 1:10 NASB).

Drat.

If I peel away the layers of my soul, way down deep, I find an excruciating longing to follow Jesus. Look how far He's taken me. Look from where He's rescued me. Look how He's dusted me off and set me on my feet two hundred and fifty bazillion times. I'm fanatically in love with Him. So if this is true, I need to shed my need-for-everyone-to-like-me coat in favor of His robe of redemption, His mantle of humble submission.

Ironically, I'm closer to Jesus through this foray into reputation bashing than I am when folks applaud me. I cling to Him because He understands. I learn the blessed importance of silence, of not defending even when I ache to. It's a beautiful thing to place my reputation in His hands, come what may.

I find solace in knowing I'm not the only one with this problem, this stronghold choking joy from my life. Recently, my friend Molly sits across from me, walking my same reputation journey, grace on her face. "I spent several years staying quiet," she whispers. "It was what God asked me to do — to let someone say all sorts of things about me, untrue things, and yet, still not defend. I'd walk into a room knowing people might've heard the rumors. All I could do was keep my mouth shut and entrust my reputation to Jesus." She shares an excruciatingly rich time of pain mingled with joy.

Molly's words resonate with me. I identify with her journey. At times I wish I don't have to follow the same path. But this path teaches me two truths.

Truth one. Jesus isn't liked by everyone. If I say I want to be a Christ follower, I have to realize I follow a disliked God-Man. If He is disliked, I will be too. Hebrews says this: "For we do not have a high priest who cannot sympathize with our weaknesses, but One who has been tempted in all things as we are, yet without sin. Therefore let us draw near with confidence to the throne of grace, so that we may receive mercy and find grace to help in time of need" (4:15–16 NASB). On earth, Jesus is tempted to be a people-pleaser, just like I am. Yet, He doesn't sin. So He can help me. Jesus walks the perfect life, yet some folks don't like Him. Even so, He maneuvers their disapproval perfectly. Which means there is hope for an approval-monger like me. Which means I can be whole without needing the masses to shout my praises. (I'm reminded of the fickleness of crowds, how on one day they chant Hosanna, the next day giving way to howls of Crucify.) Jesus has been unliked. I can be too.

Truth two. Managing my reputation with others, capitulating to the Andreas of my life, doesn't give folks the opportunity to love the real Mary. If I hound after someone's approval, jump through every hoop, I never know if that person loves me for me, or simply embraces the perfect persona I've put forth. Being fallible, needy, and human gives others the chance to love me as I am. It gives me the opportunity to experience grace even as it gives others the opportunity to extend grace. My messiness serves as a measuring stick for my relationships. Here's how.

Not long ago, I write something to a friend, then regret my words. I email right back, apologizing. Her sweet response blesses me. She writes something like, "Oh, Mary. I knew you didn't mean that. Don't give it another thought. We are sisters of grace." How her words wash over me! Her grace cleanses my worried heart. My risk in going back to my friend not only validates our friendship, but also endears me to her.

Another friend sends me an email to tell how I've wronged her. I cower in my apology, even though I'm not quite sure what I've done. I receive a virulent reply, a scathing rebuke. I so want to grovel and pour wrath upon myself after this interchange, to take what I perceive as the high road and say, "Yeah, you're right. I am awful. It's a good thing you are angry at me." I take a few deep breaths and call a friend, asking for advice. I pray. Instead of instantly responding by admitting my own worthlessness, I let it go, appreciating that my friend's response may be problematic, that it may have nothing to do with me. I don't write a response. I don't hit send. To risk being disliked, in this case, gives me great insight into the viability of this friendship.

Anne Lamott says this: "Risk being unliked. Tell the truth as you understand it. If you're a writer, you have a moral obligation to do this. And it is a revolutionary act — truth is always subversive."[4] Like Anne, I'm learning to tell the truth, even if it means folks won't like me.

Even if it means my reputation is marred.

Even if it means being silent.

Even if it means I feel alone in this world.

Even if my personal need for order and harmony are shattered. Even if.

I tell the truth because my desperate desire to be liked is a snare. My realization of this, after far too many years of striving after the wind, is a thin place where Jesus shows up. He tells me, "I've been there. I wasn't always liked." King David echoes the same sentiment: "I carry in my heart the insults of so many people" (Psalm 89:50 NLT).

Isn't it ironic that I have the deepest fellowship with Jesus when I give up my need to control the relationships in my life? My relationship with Him grows rich when I place my reputation in the hands that are scarred by the hatred of others.

A tear leaks out when I sit next to my daughter Sophie on the couch. We're watching the courtroom scene of *To Kill a Mockingbird*, where Atticus clearly proves Tom Robinson's innocence though the jury disagrees. He gathers up his papers. White folks have abandoned the ground floor of the courtroom. All except the court reporter. One by one the people in the balcony rise until one person is left sitting — Scout. The pastor behind her tells her to stand because her daddy is passing by.

For a long time after the scene, my mind reels. I place myself in the courtroom, in Atticus's shoes, though they feel awfully clunky on my skinny feet. Such big shoes to fill, really. I read Luke chapter 4 and it all comes together. Jesus lives His life first to please His Father. This endears Him to the balcony folks, but it enrages those on the floor level of this world, those in power, those whose control is threatened by His loving, firm ways. Luke 4 starts with Jesus being tempted by the Devil — a battle of control and dominion. In verse 15, we hear about Jesus, how He is "praised by all." By the end of the chapter, we read, "And all the people in the synagogue were filled with rage as they heard these things; and they got up and drove Him out of the city, and led Him to the brow of the hill on which their city had been built, in order to throw Him down the cliff" (vv. 28 – 29 NASB).

One moment, the entire courtroom cheers Jesus — the next, they want His neck broken.

What makes me cry while Scout stands is I realize I spend far too much time worrying what the folks on the lower level of the courtroom are thinking, forgetting that the real joy in life comes when I'm blessing those who don't have a voice. That's how Jesus does things. Gives justice to the orphan and widow. Stoops low to children to bless them when the disciples are too busy to be bothered. Elevates the mite of the widow over the gold of the Pharisee. Heralds the tax gatherer's sincere prayer over the self-righteous man's haughty petition.

When I get to heaven, I long to see balcony folks, applauding how Jesus touched them through small me. And then I'll join them, standing up for Jesus as He leaves the courtroom of earth.

9

Slow Dancin'

I have this terrible fascination with boys when I am in sixth grade. They repulse me, and yet I need their attention. All I really want in life is a hug from a boy or man—someone to hold me and tell me everything is going to be okay. But tangled in that fierce hunger is a fear so big I flee before a hug ever materializes.

I get my new fatty-legged jeans in the sixth grade and suddenly I am pop-U-lar. I even get invited to Kelly's exclusive party, an invitation my frizzy-haired blonde friend hasn't received. Butterflies disco in my stomach when my mom drops me off. The lights are down low in the family room. Music shouts from a brand-spanking-new 8-track player. I play along, like I am supposed to be part of this group, but inside I worry about tossing my graham crackers. Why? Because the music shifts from fast to slow, and my newfound friends are slow dancing in front of me. Bodies press themselves together in a swaying hug.

I want to leave.

Boys and men are not safe creatures. They don't want to simply console a girl who needs a Daddy. They want to take her soul, her body, her voice. Though I don't tell anyone, other than Eva the chain-smoking babysitter, I keep my secret shame perfectly hidden from view.

But I know.

As my friends hug-sway, I panic. I hover near the wall, throw my glances to the ground. Joe, the cutest, most popular boy in my class walks over to me. He taps my shoulder. "Would you like to dance?" For a moment, I catch a hint of his blue-blue eyes, his blond hair, and think maybe this wouldn't be too bad. But then I remember.

"Um, no, I don't feel well, but thanks," I stammer.

He walks away, shaking his blond head. Taking those blue eyes with him.

I scold myself for saying no, but the terror keeps me clinging to the wall.

Kelly rushes over. "You said no to Joe? Are you crazy?" He is her secret crush.

"I don't feel very well," I repeat. "Can I call my mom?"

"Sure." She hands me the phone, then retreats to the group.

I nearly bow to my mom's car when she comes early to pick me up.

Junior high sees more dancing to the tune of Bee Gees and REO Speedwagon. I attend every dance, but I stay along that safe wall, feigning interest in my cuticles. I battle inside myself, a girl longing to be loved and a girl repulsed by boys bent on stealing from me. I go home having not set foot on the dance floor, utterly devastated, feeling like a pimply, skinny mess, but also relieved that I don't have to slow dance.

I eventually get up the nerve to dance, really dance. I turn sixteen and move again, this time far away from my lingering nerdiness. At this new high school, I am a girl without identity. In my old school where chubby cheerleaders had far more merit than a scrawny girl with brains, I hardly gathered notice. In this new place, brains are cool and skinny is in. I start coming out of myself. This includes dancing.

I get myself a new do—all Flock of Seagulls in its asymmetry. I bleach the front, have my bisexual hairdresser Dallas shave the other side. I wear pegged Levis, forever banishing wide-legs to their rightful place—the land of faux-pas fashion. I attend my first dance and—God forbid!—ask boys to dance. A group of us girls go downtown to teen dance clubs where clove cigarettes and stale beer mingle on sticky dance floors. I dance until I become a string bean of sweat.

When Slater asks me to slow dance at a high school dance, I nearly jump out of my skin with surprise. Slater is a catch, to be sure—Mr. Evasive Coolness all wrapped up in one boy. He holds me close—I no longer run away. We dance to "Almost Paradise," one of those snarky songs from the *Footloose* soundtrack, which, by the way, I love because they quote Bible verses in favor of dancing. A time to dance, indeed. All weekend long after that fateful, silly dance, I nearly wear out my 45 of "Almost Paradise." I play it over and over and over and over again, imagining cool Slater holding skinny me. I keep the illusion in my mind until the next week at school, where Mr. Coolness treats me like any other silly girl he dances with.

In college, I continue dancing like a crazy woman until my well-meaning, legalistic friends convince me I am practically in bed with Satan when I dance to secular music. Satan has apparently done a lot of stuff with music and dancing since Jesus crushed his head. He's spent his time wandering to and fro throughout the earth, creating this evil, tribal beat that, if listened to, will arouse men to lust, women to fall, people to do all sorts of unspeakable acts. And if I am to be pure and holy, I really need to reconsider my love affair with dancing. Desperate to please Jesus, I quit cold turkey. I even sacrifice my evil albums—vile crooners like Lionel Ritchie and Duran Duran—and smash them to holy pieces, dumping them down my dorm garbage chute in holy triumph.

But I still want to dance. Need to. I graduate to Christian dances, where they play the same-sounding music, which now glorifies Jesus and not Satan. Except that no one really dances much. Everyone seems so nice and pure and, well, bored. To be honest, the music is lame. Something inside me deadens while I listen to Bryan Duncan screeching in that voice of his, or Amy Grant singing about fat babies. It will be many, many years before I can dance again and feel God's pleasure. The legalists succeed in draining me of joy. Even so, I am proud of my dance abstinence. Like any good legalist.

After college, I spend five weeks in Malaysia on a short-term outreach. Most of my duties center on transporting a dance team from YWAM Hong Kong from one performance to another. I get to know these dancers—sweet, edgy folks who dance for Jesus with all their might. I'll never forget sitting down cross-legged and stretching with them. One of the dancers looks at me wide-eyed. "Have you ever danced?" he asks.

"No, not really. Why?"

"You have great flexibility. Have you ever considered it?"

I smile.

My last Sunday in Malaysia, I have a vision. I don't normally have these. You can argue that since I am in a foreign country eating things like pig intestine and fish eyeballs, I am a little beaten down and in want of visions, but I see what I see. In the midst of worship, I close my eyes. Before me dances Jesus. He waves this banner-ish thing, probably because I am having my vision in a charismatic church strewn with banners, and He is dancing like a crazy man. He stops in front of me, offering the banner like an invitation. I shake my head no. He continues to dance, shorter spurts this time, always returning to me with the invitation. I'm afraid. Not the sort of afraid that worries me about Joe's advances in the sixth grace, but a holy terror of letting myself be truly free in Jesus. After all, isn't dancing sinful? Jesus and His dancing ways is a thin place for me, where I nearly kiss His presence.

With trembling hands, I take the banner and dance, letting go, reveling in Jesus as my dance partner. The vision ends. I share it with the dance team and with the pastor of the Chinese church where I am working. Both say it means I am supposed to join them — either as a dancer or a youth pastor. Though I am in that time of my life when I actively look for fleeces and signs and supernatural leadings, I choose to fly home where I'll be responsible and get a real job for goodness' sake.

Patrick and I try to dance at our wedding, but it becomes a laughable mess. We are married after a freak Northwest snowstorm. As a result, many can't come to our wedding. One of the weather casualties is a killer sound system that never arrives. Our poor soundman tries to make a terribly outdated and cheap boombox amplify music without too much static, but it is no use. So Patrick and I knock knees — though he's taller, our knees hit at the same place, a sure recipe for bruises — to static and our own awkward laughter.

I haven't thought much of dancing until the past two years or so. My mind harkens back to dancing, spinning Jesus, and a longing bursts from me. I'm no longer the girl caught in the strange dichotomy of being petrified of men, yet pining for their affections. When Jesus picks me at fifteen, He launches me on a very long journey of healing and weeping and stumbling. I am ready to dance again, ready to abandon myself to life.

It comes — my dance opportunity. The backdrop? A time of worship. Many of us spill into a small area, the music pulsing through us. We jump up and down, surfing people above our heads. I dance until I sweat through my clothes. I laugh at it all. Marvel at the beauty of life, of how deeply God redeems us. Twirling and laughing, I am no longer the frightened girl at Kelly's party, afraid of dancing, afraid of men, afraid of life. I am a woman in frenzy, one who loves Jesus with all her heart, who chooses to dance to a raucous beat, all for the sake of the One who beckoned her to dance with Him in the first place.

I never really knew a dance floor could be a thin place.

10

Kiss

The Chalet Theater once preened in our small farming town, but now its floors stick to my feet — years of Coke and 7UP mopped into its ancient DNA. Lemonheads roll down the incline toward the screen while sixth graders like me chatter, chucking the little yellow candies at each other. Which would all be fine if it weren't for Derek sitting next to me.

It's after San Francisco Riding Gear. After the slow dancing party. Though puzzled, I'm sure, by my fear of dancing, the cool girls are still wooing me to their world — a world that involves boyfriends and kissing. "Derek likes you." The note, written in typical sixth grade girl loop-de-lou writing, stares at me, makes my tongue thick in my mouth. Derek? Likes me?

He is my height with dark hair, reminding me of Eddie Munster. He smiles a lot. And he apparently likes me.

The next note arrives. "He wants to know if you will go with him." Girls flitter around me at recess, pressuring me to say yes.

"Come on. He likes you. And he's cute."

"You should go with him."

"You'll be cool if you do."

My stomach feels like it's courting the flu. I protest, but the chattering of my new friends and my desperation to fit in wears me thin. I check a box on a note, telling Derek yes, I will "go with him."

It's nearing the end of the day—a long awaited Friday afternoon—when a friend passes me another note. "He wants to kiss you at the Chalet Theater tonight. Are you going?"

My stomach flu intensifies. At the last recess, I declare, "I am not going to kiss Derek! No way! No one ever said anything about kissing."

But the queen of the cool girls pulls me aside. "You'll like it. I promise. He's really nice, and this is what you do when you go with someone. Didn't you know that? He expects it."

"But I don't want to." My voice sounds terribly unpersuasive.

She puts an arm around me. Her voice is gentle, almost matronly. "It'll be fine. I'll be there too. Really. Just come tonight."

"I don't know how."

"It's easy. Just remember to close your eyes. That's the most important part. You don't want to be caught looking cross-eyed. Like this." She bends close to me and crosses her eyes.

I laugh.

She tells me to sit. I obey.

She looks at me. "After that, he will probably try to stick his tongue—"

"His tongue?" Flashbacks of second grade at the day care roar back. A boy dared me to touch my tongue to his. At first I ran away, but eventually I bent to the dare pressure, stuck out my tongue toward his, and screamed when mine met his. Slimy. Like licking a slug.

The queen bee rolls her eyes. "Um, yeah. His tongue. It's called French kissing. So anyway, you close your eyes."

"And let him lick me?"

She laughs. "No. You open your mouth and let him in. Just like that. You don't have to know how, just let him do the kissing."

My mom drops me off at the Chalet. I run to the bathroom first, my new friends flitting around me, laughing and chattering. They treat it like any other Friday night. One by one, they ready their lips with Bonnie Bell lipgloss, bubble gum flavored. I do too, but I wish I didn't have to.

Derek, my boyfriend of seven hours, sees me in the lobby. He smiles (of course). He seems nonchalant when he takes my hand and leads me to the soiled velvet seats. Other friends surround us. For a moment we are caught in the revelry of watching previews and catapulting lemonheads. The Chalet dims its lights to nothingness.

Derek stretches his left arm around me. I tell my stomach to stop souring. As a girl newly introduced to the world of popularity and dating, I have no romantic notions about a first kiss. I'm only twelve. I haven't spent several adolescent years pining for that perfect moment, envisioning it, caressing it. The whole matter of kissing is simply a petrifying rite of passage I must step through, not anticipate joyfully. With Derek's arm weighting my shoulders, all I really want to do is make an excuse and go home, but I'm determined to get this over with, so I stay anchored to my seat.

Of all the movies playing that night, it has to be a violent bunny cartoon called *Watership Down* where rabbits go to war. Twenty or so minutes into bleeding bunnies, Derek's face is thrust in front of mine. I shriek. He jerks back. Unrelenting — that Derek wants his kiss — he leans in again. I close my eyes. Open my mouth. Let his slug-of-a-tongue in.

I'm attacked by saliva boy — a wet, long, slobbery mess. When Derek pulls away, all I want to do is wipe my lips and chin and nose. Or gargle with mouthwash. But I can't. I feel like I did when I watched the branches clash above me, but there are no tree trunks, no leaves, only the animated forests of *Watership Down*. So instead of gazing heavenward at trees, I make a strange journey. Derek kisses me several more times, but I am floating above him like a bird on a branch, removed from the spectacle below, watching twelve-year-old me get my first kiss while cartoon bunnies kill one another.

It happens again in eighth grade, in the alleyway behind the Chalet, but this time the boy has roving hands to match his tongue. I'm kissed again in tenth grade at another romantic movie: *Return of the Jedi*. As a senior by my prom date. That summer, by my camp counselor boyfriend. Then as a sophomore in college by a ski jock after a dance. I joke that I am destined to be kissed every two years. But each time, I break up with my "boyfriend" immediately after being kissed. Kissing, simply put, freaks me out.

When Patrick kisses me the first time, my stomach feels much like it did when Derek the saliva boy attacked me. But it's a different kind of stomachache—one of dancing butterflies and fairies and joy. We are watching a movie, but thankfully not at the Chalet Theater. The day before, he spends a good deal of time explaining why we cannot date. "I'm in school full time, working nights, and you live so far away," he says. We have spent several months as friends, writing letters back and forth—he in India working at Mother Teresa's Home for the Dying and Destitute, me a school-teacher in the States.

When his head obscures the movie and his lips meet mine, I don't recoil.

We both sit back, stunned. "I thought we weren't going to date," I say.

He responds with another kiss.

Six months later, he asks me to be his wife. Six months after that, we kiss on the altar, starting our lives together.

But Derek's kiss haunts me still.

Though I am fully in the moment whenever Patrick kisses me, my once-eager involvement eventually regresses. Again, I am floating above, watching him kiss me, disconnected, not passionate as I once was. My mind has skewed, believing kissing is about being taken from, rather than joyfully giving. It agonizes me that I'm hurting my husband by not engaging with him this way, that it's seldom me who initiates kisses. It's an injury I carry with me, pressing my lips together, keeping my husband out.

Perhaps it's my fear of vulnerability. Or my need for more healing. Or that Derek messed me up for life. Or that I'm still that frightened sixth grader who grew up far too soon. Or that I'm rebellious. Or, you fill in the blank.

My patient—though quite bewildered—husband walks me through my struggle with kissing. Sparks of hope ignite their way into our marriage of eighteen years, one hesitant kiss at a time, where I again learn that Patrick is not Derek, taking something from me that is precious; he is giving me something even more precious: grace, hope, unconditional love.

At five, I'm looking to the sky for redemption, for divine rescue. I am, unfortunately, engaged in what the boys do to me, but I'm looking up, beckoning for release. In sixth grade, I've flown to the sky on my own volition, saving myself by detaching from Derek's slobbery kiss. I am looking down on myself. Somewhere between twelve and forty-one, I struggle to get back on the ground, to connect with life, with those I love, once again beckoning God for release and help. I'm grieved that my way of rescuing me hasn't worked quite the way I envisioned it. Yes, I am safe flying above, but I am not kissing life.

Jesus gently reminds me that my life is hidden with Him way up high. I get it right when I'm five, looking heavenward for rescue and salvation. I take things into my own trembling hands when I fly to earth's ceiling on my own accord. Truthfully? I'm terrified to come back down to earth. Frightened to let my feet touch the ground and walk alongside those I love. Because that's where all the hurt is. And was. And will be. Isn't it better to fly?

No. Not if it means rescuing myself.

Paul says, "Set your mind on the things above, not on the things that are on earth. For you have died and your life is hidden with Christ in God" (Colossians 3:2–3 NASB). Jesus is the One who hides my life. Not me. He tells me to look to heaven, not back down on myself trying to navigate kissing.

It's strange to write that I have to trust Jesus in kissing, but it's awkwardly true. My reticence is a paradoxical thin place, where I see afresh how much like a frightened twelve-year-old I am, how completely dependent I am upon Jesus to heal me and set my feet and soul and heart on terra firma. How I need to let Patrick be the arms and hands and lips of Jesus—a gentle healer, bent on my good. Always my good.

Recently a miracle occurs. Patrick holds me, then kisses me. In what can only be described as God's handiwork, I feel myself there, in his embrace. My feet stand on the earth, my heart given to my husband, my lips tasting his. Tasting the grace and redemption of God who has rescued me. In every single way.

11

Raggedy

She haunts me sometimes, the raggedy girl. Mismatched socks, ratty hair, a skinny body averse to baths. I see black and white pictures of myself back then.

I stand on a pier, the water gray beneath me. My hair is tied back with a ribbon. I wear mismatched socks and a streak of dirt across my face.

I walk proud chested into the wind, my blonde hair stringing behind me. My white shirt is soiled, my shorts ill-fitting. I am barefooted.

I hold an ancient camera, ponytails askew. I'm sitting on the cement rim of a fountain, corduroy-clad legs dirtied from the day.

My shoulder length hair is stringy, my paisley shirt buttoned improperly, making my collar crooked. I'm sitting on a decaying fence, a cowboy hat scrunched over my hair. I smile with crooked teeth.

I wonder. Am I still that little girl? When people see me now, can they discern my raggedy roots? Does it even matter?

I watch people when I start junior high. Watch how they walk through fashion with ease, how spit-polished they are, thanks to a mom who makes sure. I especially watch Aunt Julie, who, to me, is the epitome of all things put together. When I'm blossoming into a new teenager, she takes time to spiff me up. The day after Thanksgiving, the biggest shopping day of the year, Aunt Julie patiently rolls my hair in her hot rollers.

"Your hair is a lot like mine," she says. "It's fine and needs some body." She rolls a strand of my hair and secures it with a clip. When she rolls one near my ear, she takes a piece of cotton and protects me from getting burned.

She shows me how to apply makeup. "Mascara brings out your eyes," she tells me. "And cover up under your eyes will get rid of the dark circles."

I stand tall next to Aunt Julie, trying to act put together as she is. My grandmother takes our picture, we two with umbrellas gripped tightly in front of us. We venture to Frederick and Nelson's, The Bon Marché, and Nordstrom. We eat lunch at a hotel or a fancy restaurant. For a moment, I'm a princess.

But as soon as my hair retangles, I'm back to raggedy me.

It's not only the way I look—it's my room too. Piles of "important" papers—candy wrappers, notes from friends, bits of garbage I treasure—overtake my room, causing my mom much angst. The battle of "clean your room" ensues for a good four years. My poor mother! How many headaches I cause.

Mirroring my own struggle with how I look, I shove bits of paper into corners, under my bed, in the closet, longing for order. Though I intrinsically understand that I feel much, much better when things are orderly, I can't seem to pull it all together; and when I do, it's terribly temporary.

Messy, raggedy me.

I compensate, or try to. In eighth grade I spend a year in modeling school, for a company whose motto is something like, "Be a model, or just look like one." They're such a legit firm that my mom ends up getting our registration money back in a lawsuit. I wear pumps for the first time—a teeter-tottering experience. I try to grow out my bangs. I don't smile for my headshot, so my lips cover up my braces. I goop on pancake makeup. I'm nervous most of the time, though I fit the model profile: tall and skinny. But a seediness stitches through the entire ordeal. Even before I know Jesus, I don't like the idea of being summed up by how I look. Though I battled my own sense of raggedy-ness, I can't bring myself to lay my life down for a career in modeling (not that I really could … being average looking).

I enter a pageant when I start high school, completely naïve to that world. I somehow think I might actually win the Miss T.E.E.N. (Teens Encouraging Excellence Nationally) contest. But I don't. Even though I have far better grades than my room-mate, she wins the academic category, probably because she raises the most money for the pageant. A blonde, cute, perky girl who dazzles us all with her Americana piano concerto wins the whole thing. During the "evening gown" presentation, I wear the dress my grandmother made me of (gasp!) a shiny mauve rose fabric, with lace aplenty. I sing "On Broadway" in a fake tux. Embar-rassing. Even during the pageant, I realize I'm not quite put together—that my clothing choices, the way my hair behaves, and my "poise" all need making over.

Instead of trying to figure it out—something that seems impossible to me at the time—I give up.

At the same time, my soul feels tattered too. I'm in that place of over-disclosure, where I tell my life tale of woe to any listening ear. I wonder how many people run from me, screaming, smart-ing from disclosure fatigue. I can't help but talk. Now I see it as the way God made me to deal with all the baggage. I picture Him in heaven, knitting me together in my mother's belly. "This one will need the gift of words. It'll come in handy someday," He proclaims. And it's true. It comes in handy all right, but in high school I'm far too inexperienced to wield my words with finesse. Instead, I spew my raggedy soul on folks.

I attempt to change in college, try to make a fresh start of things. God gives me a beautiful, amazing friend who has fashion sense aplenty and a string of young men lining up at her door, begging for dates. I stand off to the side, trying to glean. More times than I can count, I field inquiries from guys I like — questions like, "Do you think she'll go out with me?" or "Is she busy this weekend?" or "Do I have a chance?" Though it irks me, I love my friend so much that I get over myself.

My dorm room is blessedly clean, and my clothes aren't as messy as they used to be. I'm growing up.

I live in California for a summer during college. I revel in the freedom of being far away from home, able to do the thing I love so much: youth ministry. Though it is a fascinating adventure, one cloud hangs over it.

On a short visit, my mom says, quite matter of fact, "My daughter's messy." She points to the kitchen floor in the place my roommate and I are staying. She bends low, sweeps up some crumbs with her hands, then swats them into the garbage bin's mouth. I'd intended to harvest those renegade crumbs, but I'd been too late.

My roommate laughs. Really laughs. "Yeah, you're right."

My mom means nothing by it. My roommate, either. I tell myself that. I sweep the comment away and try to swat it into the dustbin, but those words cling to me like grease on a stovetop. I've felt that way my whole life. Messy. You wouldn't know it now if you walk into my home. I love order, simplicity, cleanliness. Ironically, my mom's comment is no longer true, yet I hold onto it, clasp it to my heart, believe it, let it fester.

I look at pictures of me as a little kid and marvel at God's work. My messy clothes are simply a symptom of what abides inside me: chaos, fear, worry, insecurity. He's revamped my soul — ushering me into a place of acceptance with myself, making me unashamed of my upbringing.

Now I'm not so traumatized by raggedy Mary. Because, in some ways, I still am raggedy. Though God has delivered me from my inner chaos, there are still crumbs all over the floor of my soul. Under the bed of my heart live dust bunnies of pride, worry, wrath, and fear. But God loves messy me anyway.

My internal messiness is a thin place for me where I realize God loves messy. He delights in my raggedy ways. Why? Because He redeems my messes. Cleans them up. Polishes them until they shine so bright the reflection of Jesus smiles back. Paul affirms this. He says, "We have this treasure in earthen vessels, so that the surpassing greatness of the power will be of God and not from ourselves" (2 Corinthians 4:7 NASB).

Clean shiny folks don't have the sacred privilege of understanding God's greatness or power because they're so full of their own beauty. Messy folks understand the metaphor of an earthen vessel, a clay pot, a canister that holds refuse. And, in that humble state of mess-dom, we welcome the beauty of Jesus within.

So, yeah, I'm a raggedy mess. But God loves the socks off me anyway. I'm a cracked pot, a vessel God shines His loveliness through. Thank goodness for the cracks; otherwise how would God's glory shine out?

I remake the California picture in my mind. I stand in the kitchen, crumbs about my feet. Jesus enters, nods to my roommate. He stoops to the floor, brushes the crumbs into His hand, kisses them, and blows them to the wind. "I love messy," He says with a wink and a jig. Throwing my arms around Him, I shout amen.

∾

One morning on my run, I feel the hand of God upon me. The night before, I have a little revelation from Jesus about myself: particularly, how I've forgotten Him, how I've conveniently pushed Him aside while I accomplish my own agenda, leaving me selfish and self-absorbed. So I cry out to Jesus. "Show me Yourself."

A litany of offenses parade in front of me. I realize how very, very weak I am, left to my own devices. I don't capture the time with my kids like I should. I nag my husband instead of praying for him. I place my own agenda above others. I live selfishly.

In the next breath, I remember the sins committed against me.

Oh, how frail I am. Oh, how weak. Oh, how much I need the grace of God. The Lord whispers, "Your weakness is the platform for forgiveness." So true! It's easier for me to see my own need for grace than to see that folks who hurt me have that same weakness and need. We're messy ragamuffins, all of us. If I dare enter Jesus' presence asking for grace for my own sin (because of my weakness), then I can certainly grant that others battle the same weakness. My humanness helps me to forgive.

I'm flawed. Helplessly selfish. Needy. Clay-footed. When I see myself thus, and experience the wild grace of God on my behalf, my very unworthiness helps me offer the same grace to fellow strugglers. It's a good thing to be messy sometimes, particularly when that messiness produces heaps of empathy.

I type this in my bathrobe, hair askew, breath bad, teeth sweatery. I'll clean up after I'm done with my word count, and that's okay. Because I'm learning that God loves me as I am, that I'm no longer defined by my messy appearance or a paper-strewn office. I'm defined by the God who dared to be messy Himself with people, leaving the perfection of heaven for the dirtiness of earth —who went on a holy mission to rescue raggedy folks like me.

12

Narcissism

Riding in my mom's car, I'm a bit morose thinking she's forgotten my thirteenth birthday. The transition from girl to woman should be celebrated with more than a simple present and a happy birthday song sung at breakfast. As an only child, I revel in birthdays and Christmases because so many presents are directed my way, heightening my expectations. But today seems different. I am forgotten.

She gets out of the car. I follow. We're at a large suburban mall with restaurants flanking its white-bricked perimeter. One restaurant is Farrell's, an ice cream emporium that hosts my favorite ice cream sundae: a FudgeAnna Banana. She is nonchalant as she opens the door. "Well, since it's your birthday," she tells me, "we may as well stop in and get you your favorite sundae."

We look for a seat. Echoes of "surprise" startle and surprise me all at once. A surprise party. Just for me. All for me.

Sometimes I wonder if I have NPD: Narcissistic Personality Disorder. I've had my share of run-ins with people like this, whose lives revolve solely around themselves. I'm left feeling crazy, confused, and blaming myself for an infraction I'm not sure I've done. One woman blames me for her screaming. Another elevates her parenting as superior and I'm left feeling like an unfit mother.

But even worse is the insidious worry that attacks me when I think about NPD. Do I have it? Does the world revolve around me, or do I think it should? Am I a person of sacrifice or selfishness?

In the third grade, I am standing in the doll aisle of an Ohio department store with my grandmother Mary, the one whose grave I stand over in the beginning of this book. Thin lips pressed together, she says, "No, Mary. We're not going to buy you a doll today."

I cross my arms across my chest and fly into tears. Then I run. Away.

The store employees make a frantic search.

In my hands I'm clutching her — the small bald-headed doll with a yellow dress.

My grandmother finds me. Exasperated, she throws her cash on the counter and buys me that doll. I cradle her the rest of my visit, while the world revolves around me.

As I get older, will I turn into one of those people who can't see beyond herself, who spews her ache-and-pain-of-the-day, demanding instant help? Will I disregard others? Or blame them for my own sin?

It's a fear I can't seem to wash away. When I read through my journals that span the few years after I meet Jesus, I see a me who is more selfless, seemingly more in tune with Jesus' presence. I read my prayers of agony, longing to see my friends meet Jesus. I view every day as a holy event, an opportunity to serve someone else. I read how I find a homeless man, rush to McDonald's to buy him lunch, only to find him gone afterwards. I chase that poor man down in my car, handing him his cold food. In a park-and-ride, I see a woman in a car. I believe Jesus wants me to talk to her, so I do. She looks at me with mild amusement as I stutter a few Jesus words her way. As told, I try to pick up a crazy hitchhiker woman who careens her way into the middle of the road. She freaks me out, so I drive on by, feeling guilty. In the days of back then, I'm Super Christian, doling out selfless acts like Lifesavers.

But now I'm older. And wiser? And less self-absorbed? I've circled the wagons of my heart. I'm weary of pain, weary of engagement, weary of putting myself out there. So I spend time in self-protect mode. I guard my time. I guard my relationships. I am miserly with my affections. And I take few servanty risks.

As a young teen I visit nursing homes. People seem to fall into three categories: those with serious dementia or health problems, those who are bitter and angry, and those who exude tender joy. I start formulating a theory that maybe people become more like themselves the older they get. If they're a little ornery when they're young, they're ravenously angry when they're nursing-home bound. If they're sweet and kind, they emulate love when they're older.

Will I be a narcissist when I'm eighty? Will I circle the wagons of my heart so much that I no longer grow in love?

I hope not.

Truth is, I don't like me when I'm all about me, pining for the world to throw me unending surprise parties at Farrell's.

My pastor in college shares some interesting words — the kind that stick in a craw in your brain and won't let go. Earwig thoughts. He says the best way to combat selfishness is to minister in the opposite spirit. He says it works in anything, really. If you're stressed about money, give it away. If someone takes you down with his words, take him down with your kindness. Maybe that works with me too. If I'm sitting — to use an old Young Life analogy — on the throne of my life, then to do the opposite would mean bowing low to another throne. If I'm absorbed in my own pursuits, then I need to become absorbed in something outside of me.

The idea further develops when I wake from a dream. Words resonate through me like God is speaking and I need to listen. I turn them around in my mind, much like I'd roll a lozenge on my tongue. Clean. Dirty. Heart. Hands.

What does God want with all these words? And which one am I? Am I clean? Dirty? Have my hands and heart been selfish or selfless?

So often, I'm of the clean-hands variety, cloistered away from the pain of this life, insulating myself from the world's mess. I can't bear to see pictures of invisible children from Rwanda. Darfur sickens me and I turn away. Poverty in Texas is far from my little suburb. My hands are clean. I'm blessedly free to think of me, absorbing myself in meeting our monthly budget, getting enough time to write, sleeping in on Saturdays.

What does living with clean hands do to my heart? I think of Mother Teresa's words about Jesus often wearing the distressing disguise of the poor. Have I missed seeing Jesus in this world because I avoid the uncomfortable truth that sin has ravished this world?

The truth? My heart is clean when I'm near Jesus Christ. And He is often found in distressing disguises. My hands need to get dirty to see Him in those thin places. My heart needs to shed selfishness, to fling off its NPD tendencies. My eyes need to be opened to Jesus and His many, many disguises.

I see Jesus at the supermarket. He bags my groceries. He appears as an addled man who bellows HELLO and I HAVE MISSED YOU and IT IS GOOD TO SEE YOU AGAIN and I SURE HOPE YOU HAVE A LOVELY DAY. He bags my items and walks them to my car. I thank the grocery man. He shuts the back of my van, as if he knows my arm can't do it. I love Jesus for that.

God is interested in the great reversal. Not clean hands and a dirty heart, but a clean heart with dirty hands. It reminds me of this verse: "Religion that God our Father accepts as pure and faultless is this: to look after orphans and widows in their distress [dirty hands] and to keep oneself from being polluted by the world [clean heart]" (James 1:27, brackets mine).

But I'm afraid I love sanitization in both parts. Clean heart. Clean hands. Clean lives. No messiness. Predictableness. (Oh how I preach to myself!) I need courage to dirty my hands, to mess up my life with the concerns of others. I need God's intervention to take my gaze away from my belly button, to minister in the opposite spirit in selflessness.

My son Aidan gets this instinctively. His compassion for the world brings me to tears. "Mom," he tells me at the beginning of sixth grade, "I want to run for Class Treasurer."

I pound out his speech onto the computer while he dictates it to me. He really has only one point, so he struggles to add two more. "I want to be treasurer so I can help fund wells in Africa," he says. "I don't think it's fair to have people walk miles and miles for clean water."

When he steps off the bus on election day, his head is down.

"I didn't win." His voice sounds pinched. He sits on my bed, fighting tears. "It's not fair," he says.

"I know," I tell him. "I've lost plenty of elections. It just plain stinks, doesn't it?"

"You don't understand." He shifts on the bed, and then looks at me with his daddy's eyes. "I have this vision I can't get out of my head — for those people in Africa who don't have fresh water. Now I can't help them!"

How misplaced my words are. I assume he's sad that he's not been chosen, but instead he's grieving for the people in

Africa—folks he's never met. Aidan is the opposite of narcissism. And I love that about him. I love his tenacity too. Despite his political setback, he finds a way to raise money for a new well.

Maybe that's why God gives some of us children. To bring us back to Him. To see the world through Jesus-colored glasses. I confess: I navel-gaze. I self-protect. I pull my life in, forgetting to look out. My hands are often clean.

But not always anymore. Aidan is my divine revelation that won't let me forget who I was back then. He is God's pop-up window to keep me dirtying my hands with the mess of this world. My son's compassion is a thin place that enables me to see Jesus' compassion. Sitting on the bed, hearing Aidan pour out his heart, I feel the presence of Jesus. It's enticing. It's overwhelmingly inviting.

Even to a narcissist like me.

13

Singing

Although I sing Olivia Newton John constantly, my typical audience is the open skies and my three-legged German shepherd.

The seventh grade choir director eyes us all and asks, "Who of you would like to go to Contest?" The Diva of seventh grade — who knows well her diva status — says no.

I raise a shaky hand. No one here knows I sing. I'm not even sure I know I sing — at least not in a contesty sort of way. Weeks later, I stand in front of the choir and sing about the sound of music, how the hills are alive with it. I sing it clear, hitting every note. I sing it loud, my voice reverberating off the back wall of our ancient auditorium. Surprised choir members clap. My choir teacher smiles.

When I stand in front of the judges at Contest, I know they must expect a willowy, wispy voice from a thin girl like me. I take a breath and let out each note, clear and bold. They smile and tally their votes. I jump up and down when I see the 1 marked at the top of the tally sheets — a superior.

I tell no one that all I really want is to win the Outstanding Girl Soloist Award, the award everyone thinks the Diva will win. Shy, overlooked kids come up to me. "I voted for you," they say. I tally their votes in my head, while the rest of our choir congratulates the Diva on the award before it's presented. When the choir teacher calls my name instead, I stand on shaky legs. Grabbing that award, I cannot remember a time in my life before this when I felt so happy.

Singing saves me. It steadies me and connects me with God through high school and college. In my twenties, I realize I'll never be a famous singer, and I'm okay with that. I relegate my longing for fame to singing on worship teams, which works just fine —until I attend a gigantic church with a professional sounding team. When I try out, I'm stuffed up from a cough and cold and miss notes. The audition becomes a noose around my happiness, choking it clear out. I still relive the humiliation in my mind.

In France, I lead worship—my dream realized—only to find out it's no longer the joy I once thought it would be. When I'm leading, I don't have the opportunity to let go, to abandon myself to singing praise to God. It becomes work, part of a pedestrian to-do list. And besides, others in our community can lead—others whom I gladly hand the reins over to.

I'm coming to see the ebb and flow of gifting in my life. I believe God gives me a voice for a specific purpose: so that I'll be able to handle the complexities and perplexities of life. But now I'm grown up, and I cope in myriad other ways. I am learning to be content whether someone calls my name to sing, or they don't. I am letting go of my dream.

Our big church is again holding vocal auditions. I fight myself back and forth with a longing to sing for Jesus on that stage and a recognition that my time has passed. I want to sign up. My daughter tells me I should. My husband says I shouldn't. I battle the shoulds and shouldn'ts in my head, remembering how many times Jesus delivers me when I sing. Maybe He can deliver others too? But I let the deadline pass, and I let it all go.

As I mourn the loss of singing, I forget that I can still sing whenever I want. That a microphone doesn't validate my life or make my song sweeter to Jesus.

I send my worship leader friends a quick note of encouragement about a particular song they sing for the congregation, thanking them for their faithfulness. Neither knows my personal struggle. They don't know I almost tried out again. But the wife emails me back with these words: "You are a blessing to me each week as I watch you worship our great God. He uses you to encourage me." I nearly cry when I read her message. My own worship from the audience blesses the one who leads us in worship.

That's enough for me. It may not have been enough during my frenzied need to be on stage, but it's plenty today. I sing a song today. I sing it loud. I sing it strong. To the God who gave me the voice to do so — He who delivers me in song, who will yet deliver me.

Singing is one of my purest thin places, where I hear God, feel Him, am wooed by Him. I am moved more through music than any other artistic venture. Songs transport me to a time when I am as odious as a dead skunk in the middle of the road, to mountain trails as I walk side-by-side with my daddy, to angst-filled adolescence where my voice defines me, to the painful place of broken dreams. The Bible tells me God gives me songs of deliverance, and I believe it. It says He sings with joy over me. I pray that is so. It must be, because I delight in singing over my children. God gives me songs I'll never sing for an audience — songs for His ears only as I belt them in the shower in an empty house.

Though I leave worship leading behind, I sing with joy today.

I sing crazy songs that make my children belly laugh.

I lift my arms to the sky, crooning about God's faithfulness.

I teach my children harmonies.

In the car, I shower Jesus with love songs, my affection pouring out like unbroken worship.

In the shower, I lament my day in song while minor key melodies stir my heart into major key declarations of Jesus' faithfulness.

In and through it all, the sound track of my life changes. From Broadway to beach tunes, Hollywood to Handel, eighties punk to worship band praise, I belt my praise to the heavens, realizing God has called me on a new path to sing for Him unashamed, out loud and in harmony with His voice.

14

Divorce

God hates divorce. I know why. It rips children apart.

I sum up my mom's three divorces with two words placed in a line of three: grief, relief, grief.

The gist of the first divorce is a mysterious puzzle. Mom and Jim marry. Not long after, Mom and Jim divorce, although no one will really tell me exactly how old I am when the decree is made. All I know is that when I draw pictures of my family, I'm never really sure what to draw. A mom and a daughter? Two smiling parents and a child in some sort of hopeful aspiration? A stick-figure child alone? A crayon black jagged line between the mom and father with a child in the middle, a sad expression on her face?

I visit Jim on weekends. He lavishes attention on me, tells me I'm smart and delightful and creative. It's hard for me to go home where I rarely hear words like that. Jim is tall, looming in the sky above. He holds my hand. I sit on his shoulders, placing my hands on his bald head. I write him stories. I color pictures on the back of his discarded manuscripts. He displays them.

He lives in a rented house that looks like the Munster's home, except that it needs more remodeling. No dog Spot lives under the stairs, but a plethora of boxes and rats live in the dark, dank basement. The house is sliced in two, the top floor for one tenant, the middle floor for my father, and the basement, a junk-lover's paradise. This is not his home, but he seems to believe part of it is his. The owner is a stooped-over woman named Eleanor.

Jim doesn't have much money, so he becomes very creative with the way we spend our time. We shop in the basement.

I'm not sure why I believe a monster lives there. Maybe my father has enlarged my imagination to believe such things. We creep down the back stairs. The smell of must greets us when we land on the damp pavement. I cannot see the windows, though they do exist, hiding behind boxes. Jim pulls the dirty white string hanging from the dark ceiling. A small bulb lights our adventures. We sift through boxes stacked taller than three of me, looking for treasures. A cup. A stuffed animal from decades ago. Old papers. Photos of strangers. My heart sounds alarm in my ears when I hear the skittering of rat's feet through the maze of boxes. We sift until the noise gets too much, or until my father finds his treasure.

I have one relic from that time: a purloined ashtray. It's jade green with brass cigarette rests. I know it's made in China because that's what it says on the back. The piece serves as a poignant reminder of my atypical father, who steals his landlady's things and calls it adventure.

Despite our adventurous forays, Jim is not there for the in-between times. When I skin my knee and my mother places a bandage on it. When I eat dinner around the table, slurping spaghetti into my hungry mouth. When I talk to my imaginary friend. When those boys take me away. He is not there because they have signed a piece of paper saying living with each other in Eleanor's duplex is no longer an option, but I don't understand parents living in two homes. I don't think I ever will.

He says she broke his heart, abandoned him.

She says he tried to make an object out of her, filming her.

Somewhere between the he-said-she-said is a modicum of truth.

But I am left with grief. And the wonder of what could have been.

My mom meets another man while doing laundry. They marry. He is not an attentive man with kind eyes like Jim. He doesn't praise my artwork or take me shopping in basements. He digs my mom. He loves to get high. He doesn't like me. I am a nuisance, and he tells me so. When he raises his voice, I tremble. I run to my room and close the door. He wears white T-shirts, soiled from engine grease, and ripped-up hippie jeans. Often he is bare-chested. I do not remember his face, only the feeling I get in my stomach when he rampages. Within a year — that same year the boys take me out back — they are divorced. I exhale relief.

When I'm in first grade, my mom and another man move in together. Eventually they marry. He is the man who sees me every day, who helps me with homework, who reads me stories. He works hard. But he likes to party too.

When Jim dies, I consider changing my last name to my stepdad's. He is my father now, and I need him. In sixth grade, he works swing shift while my mom pursues a Master's degree. They're seldom home. But I am. Alone. A lot. For two years. And when they are together, I feel the tension in the house, wearing it like a sick expression on my lonely face. All is not well between them. I hear their fights.

In eighth grade, I sense something is terribly wrong. Though I don't know the details, I know the truth: they will leave each other. I spend most of that year crying in my counselor's office at school. He has given me a special get-out-of-class-free card I can use whenever I feel the tears pushing forward. He listens to me.

Hears my suicidal words. Wouldn't killing myself be easier than enduring what will come? How many fathers can one girl lose and be okay? Three seems to be the straw that will break my back, my will, my heart. Although I truly want to off myself, this fatherlike counselor saves my life.

But not long after, my heart breaks as swift as a brittle stick under a booted foot. It all begins with an invitation.

"Let's go out to dinner," my stepdad offers.

He picks a new restaurant in our little town. I'm thrilled to get out and have a nice meal.

He fidgets in the booth across from me, won't find my eyes. He takes a drink of ice water.

"Your mom is seeing someone else," he says. Just like that.

I swallow. My food tastes like the sawdust that lines our horses' stalls. I want to spit it out, but can't. It's been our suspicion for a long time, that her long absences from home have a reason. But hearing that it's true deflates my will. I'd hoped that my speculations would be found blessedly wrong. I hoped I'd have to apologize to my mom for thinking such a thing. But now, she would have to do the apologizing.

The waiter brings our salads. My fork stays on the left of the plate. So does my stepdad's.

"I had her followed. Several times. After work she'd go to his house." He tells me the man's name.

I look away, tears clouding my vision. Hearing that name makes me want to chuck my salad plate across the restaurant so it'll shatter in as many pieces as my heart. I want to scream every swear word I never gave myself permission to whisper. He has a name. And my mom is leaving me behind, lonely in a big farmhouse to be with that disembodied name. Not with me. Not with my stepdad. With him.

"It means we're probably getting a divorce."

"No," I whisper. "It must be a mistake. She wouldn't do that."

"She would. She did. I had undercover officers follow her, Mary. It's true." His voice sounds eerie to me then. Not familiar, but terribly distant—like he's speaking these words to an empty tiled room. He's already fading from my life, I can feel it. Detaching. Getting ready to pack his things for a new life without me.

My throat burns; my heart rips. Despair roots itself in me when I suspect something during my junior high years, then emerges in the light of that nondescript restaurant booth. It blossoms at my grandparents' home when I realize my parents' marriage is truly dead.

I am sitting on my grandparents' hearth. It's Father's Day. We've had a barbecue and are now inside the living room, recapping the day. My relatives are sitting around, laughing, talking about nothing in particular. If a stranger came in off the street and observed the interchange, they'd think it a convivial affair, a nonchalant family with no secrets.

I watch my stepfather. He is looking out the window, his eyes on horizons I'll never see. He will leave my life in a few weeks as lawyers wet their ink on divorce papers. He will walk out into that horizon, but I won't be holding his hand.

One tear drips out. Another leaks. I put my face in my hands and suck in air, heaving oxygen in and out of my lungs, barely making a noise. Tears spill through my parted fingers. Fatherless again.

My mom sees me first. "What are you crying about?" Her words have a hysterical edge to them. Her tone accuses me of being too dramatic, too needy, too hard to parent, too much in the way.

"I—"

She repeats, "Answer me. What are you crying about?"

I look at her, bewildered. I place my hands on my knees and gaze into her eyes, but she lifts hers above mine, never meeting me there. "It's Father's Day," I say. "And I'm losing another one."

She raises her voice, but I look at the world beyond the window my stepdad's found refuge in. She is saying words, but I can no longer hear them. I cry more, tumults of tears I cannot contain any longer.

My grandmother grabs my mom by the arm, pulls her into the kitchen. From the room next door, I hear her matronly voice gather steam. "You have no right to accuse her right now," she scolds. On and on, my grandmother throws words my mother's way, defending me, while I cry in the other room and the relatives try their best to comfort me. I know I've created an awkward scene in a family that rarely speaks openly about issues. I am revealing all our closeted skeletons through my grief—a grief that's become a teeming, festering wound that won't be ignored. So I'm petted. Hugged. Given water.

"You will stay here, darling," my grandmother tells me. Her face is red. "For a few days while things settle."

I am relieved, but panicked too. My mom won't look at me. I have made her look bad, and I will pay by her distance. My stepdad shoots a worried gaze my way, an I'm-sorry I feel in my gut. His last I'm-sorry before the distance between us grows in miles—he in one apartment, me in the farmhouse, alone with my mom.

They look at each other as they gather their things, wrath exchanged in glances.

As my mom and stepdad leave, I feel sick inside. They look as if they will kill each other, the anger boiling and swirling around them like an angry aura. I worry that I will be the cause of a murder suicide, all because I couldn't keep my tears from spilling out and making my grief known.

Grief. Relief. Grief.

During a difficult night in my own marriage, I slip into the rooms of my children. We have been careful never to say "divorce," but even though it will never be an option, its lure feels strong tonight. Julia is in a crib, her face scrunched into the sheets, her breathing steady. A fluff of blonde hair, like mine at her age, beckons me to pet it. I do. I smooth her hair away from her face, feel her warmth, her life, her breath like a whisper against my trembling hand. I let out the air I'm holding inside. Tears chase each other down my cheeks. She is probably how old I am when my mom and Jim divorce.

Aidan is curled into a ball on his toddler bed. Clutched between chubby arms is his wooden train—hardly a snuggly toy, but he is stubborn and must sleep with the block of wood every single night. He is three years old. He worships his older sister and tolerates his younger. And he loves his mommy and daddy. I touch his hair, run my fingers through it. I cannot walk away from a boy so small. Can't imagine severing a marriage, knowing what that would do to my sweet little boy.

Sophie's brown hair tangles around her face, the covers straightjacketing her six-year-old body. She is sweaty—a hot sleeper like her father. I watch her breathe, wonder at her dreams. I touch her wet forehead. She is how old I am when my mom divorces for the second time. She has her whole life ahead of her. A life of wonder, I hope.

I stand a long time in the kids' rooms, watching them dream innocent dreams. I am all three of them, yet I'm longing for their innocence, experiencing the ravages of divorce so young. While tears wet my face, I make a choice for my children. Patrick and I may have issues to work through, but none are so large that they're worth ripping our children apart and setting them on the empty trajectory I did not choose to walk.

I shut each door and say a prayer. Keep us together, Lord. Keep us together.

15

Suicide Poetry

I find the poem today, which really surprises me because I'm not looking for it. Tucked into an old journal, folded in fourths, a ratty piece of notebook paper, the three holes ripped from a notebook long ago. I title the piece "Prayer of the Hopeless." It's dated March 5, 1982, eight months before I meet Jesus, but during the time I'm learning more and more about Him through my Young Life leaders. It's bad poetry, written by a ninth grade girl who wants to die:

Lord, please be patient
Please take time
To understand this life of mine
I've wanted to obey You
I really have tried
To understand Your love inside
I thank You for listening
I thank You for life
I hope You understand as I take this knife
Too many rules
Too many nights

Of lonely thinking, of unseen frights
Life is too hard
And death is an escape
From life, murder and the numbness of rape
I don't want to live
I can't take it anymore
Only bad thoughts my head does store
So I'm sorry, Lord
I'm sorry, my friends
I tried to obey, but it drove me to the end
My life I have taken
The rules I have broken
For I no more can live again.

I write this at the very end of myself, a year after my family plays tug-of-war with me, my mom pulling one way, my stepdad the other. I'm left holding the severed rope. The aftermath of my grief is the lines of poetry pressed into blank paper.

I show my aunt the poem. I want her to think it beautiful, though now I'm not sure why. "I don't want to read it again." She hands it back to me, her hands white and smoothed with clean-smelling lotion. "It's too disturbing."

"It's about someone else," I lie. "Like another character."

Her eyes smile sadly. She nods. She knows better.

I wonder what God thinks when He reads it. I wonder if He hides medicine from me or dulls the knives in our drawer. I wonder how He protects me from myself during that dark, lonely year.

Thank God I'm too chicken.

Thank God He plops Young Life into my lap as I write that poem.

Thank God for good friends who listen to me cry and rant and question.

Thank God He puts inside me an innate desire to succeed rather than rebel, or who knows where I would end up.

Thank God He sends nary a boyfriend my way during this time. My gaping, oozing, festering father wound would take any interested boy into my heart, hoping for any kind of bandage to stop the bleeding. I am ripe for affection. Any kind.

When I write the poem, I am utterly lost, completely bereft of the ability to save myself. It's a cry to the God I don't yet know, but hope He knows me anyway. The poem is the thinnest of membranes between earth and heaven, a plea for Someone to stop my hand, to notice me, to be the Daddy I've longed for. Of all the prayers I could have prayed, this is perhaps the most honest. Raw, penciled words touch the page, yes, but they write their way into God's throne room.

I'm fuzzy on the theology of prayers by folks who aren't Christ followers. Does God hear them? Or not? Does He hear my suicide poem as prayer? However it plays out, I rest in God's omniscience and sovereignty. He knows it all. He sees it all. He reads my poem before I even bleed it onto notebook paper. His great plan will not be thwarted.

It takes me a lifetime to work out the words of my suicide poem. For a long time, I feel God doesn't understand me, or that He forsakes me when He decides to place me in the family I find myself in. Why? What purpose? If I were God, though I'm glad I'm not, I wouldn't allow little girls to be raped. I want them to grow up in stable, loving homes where they don't experience emotional abandonment. But I'm not God, and I don't hold everyone's individual plans in my hand like a giant earthy weaving. I see only me—a sadly myopic view.

My stubborn, self-savvy heart will not reach for the sky if my earth becomes everything I need. If people fill me up, then where is my need for the transcendent? If everything is glory and beauty and sweetness and light, will I be the type of soul that reaches to Jesus?

I come to Jesus because I need Someone who won't leave me. My poem cries for that. I sense the loneliness etched between every line. My suicide poem is simply the state of my heart without God, and He uses that desperation to woo me to Himself.

And even more than that, He makes something beautiful out of the me who wants to end myself. Instead, He creates many beginnings, many once-upon-a-times in my life. He does this to show His power, aptly displayed on the platform of my weaknesses.

For a good long year, I want to kill myself.

But now I want to live. Really live. To follow Him out of the box of my loneliness and insecurities, to find abundance when my soul lacks. Today, someone blesses me with words that help me see that God has indeed created something beautiful in me, just when I worry I've lost passion for Him. She writes, "Mary, you only think your passion has ebbed. It is clear in everything you write. It shouts its aches, its joys, its courage, and its determination. It is there. Oh so there."

I am no longer fifteen years old, penning death poetry, grieving fathers.

I'm blessedly alive to feel the wind on my face, to experience the achingly beautiful words of my children, to see Jesus in the cracks and fissures of my life.

At one time I want to die; but with my Savior inside me, today I want to live.

16

Shame

Early on, my father dulls me to the dangers of pornography. It starts with his penchant for nudity, the way he assumes it to be perfectly normal. In one black and white picture, I am sitting nude on his friend's lap — a man who is also naked — reading a story. My father asks me to bathe him, to wash his back, to pour water on his head, all while he is stark naked in his claw-foot tub. He shows me myriad pictures he takes of unclothed women — some I recognize as his girlfriends, others I don't. I remember one slew of pictures he's particularly proud of: a series of photos where women pose in his bathtub, bubbles surrounding their parts of flesh like the Puget Sound surrounds the San Juan islands.

I cringe when he sells some of these black and whites mounted on tag board at his quirky garage sale.

One picture haunts me still. I am standing outside completely naked next to my terrified friend. I must be nine years old, the age my youngest daughter is now. Making the correlation between her sweet innocence and me back then brings tears to my eyes. I remember when the picture is taken. We are at someone's house near a beach — a wild tangle of grounds that a gaggle of kids try to conquer. We scour the beach. We make faces when the adults say they're making clam spaghetti. And as dusk nears, my friend, another girl my age, and I decide to be naked. Am I the instigator? My father? I doubt it's my friend because I can see the look of horror on her face in the picture my father takes of us.

Old growth evergreens stand behind us. We are skinny and pale in the shrinking light. She wears shock on her face, her eyes wild with shame. She is covering herself up as best as she can, but she has only two hands. The contrast between us is night and day. I wear no such shocked expression. My face is serene, like the Virgin Mary in renaissance paintings. I cover myself because my friend does; but because my father has normalized nudity, I look as if I'm watching the Brady Bunch on TV. Just another day with my father snapping pictures.

That photo captures how I have been groomed to think it's entirely normal to be nine and naked with my friend. As nine turns to ten, then pre-adolescence turns to adolescence, the rape at five and this normalcy of nudity boils inside me like a witch's brew. And I start an addictive journey. It begins in fifth grade when I follow a group of kids from school to an attic where piles of pornography woo me into a dirty addiction.

I'm fourteen or fifteen, coming off a difficult visit where my grandmother discovered me with my uncle's dirty magazines. Crippled by the shame and guilt, I spent a good twenty-four hours in my grandmother's guest room emotionally beating myself up. I miss my mom every summer I fly to Ohio to see my father's parents. Something about leaving home wears on me. So after this especially difficult visit, I fly home, anxious to see her, to catch up.

But she doesn't smile when she greets me at the gate. And on the way home from the airport, my mom clears her throat. "I'm so embarrassed," she says.

"Why?"

"We pulled all the wallpaper off your walls and installed new Sheetrock," she says. "Imagine my shock when we found those books behind your bed."

I cower in the car's bucket seat. Mortification is not a word I use lightly, but in this instance, it is not strong enough. I want to die. I want to open the car door and fling myself onto the freeway so the world can be done away with me. Ugly, ugly me.

"You can just imagine how embarrassed I was, especially since my boyfriend was with me. He was shocked too."

I don't speak. When we arrive home, I cower into my room, the weight of my addiction to dirty books and awful magazines weighing so heavy on me I want to vomit. People arrive for a boisterous party.

I hear their revelry, feel hunger growl in my stomach, but I don't leave my room — my self-imposed exile. I am a filthy girl, worth nothing, wearing shame like a death shroud. That night I'm so ready to die that I feign death. I sprawl my skinny body across the floor of my room, leaving the door to my room cocked so someone will find me that way. Maybe it's my way of doing penance, though I don't even know what that word means. My mom walks by my room, probably throwing up her arms at my drama-queen ways. Eventually, a partygoer stoops into my room and asks if I'm okay. I lie and say I am tired, that I must've fallen asleep on the floor.

I can still feel the weight of my shame twenty-six years later. Never once did I consider why those books and magazines drew me. Only later, after sharing this excruciating story with my husband, do I think rationally about it.

"Where did you get the books?" he asks.

"They were my parents' books."

He raises an eyebrow. "So you read the books you found in your house."

"Yeah."

"Mary, did it ever occur to you that your parents shouldn't have had those books around in the first place?"

I peel away the entire scene after this interchange, seeing it with new eyes. Here I am, a girl who's been sexually abused, exposed to pornography, without Jesus. I am walking the path of destruction, and my own home provides the necessary stumbling blocks. I have far too much alone time in my home, the only child of working parents. And yet, it's all my fault? Sure, I take a hefty portion of the blame. I could've chosen to walk away. I wish I would have. But as I relive this scene in my mind, I wonder if things could've ended differently.

Shame is a terrible taskmaster, even a worse friend. But I've held Shame close, as boss and confidant. Though my addiction to dirty books and magazines eventually ended, thanks to Jesus, I still feel its inky blackness when I recall this story. I am so terribly frail. So clay-footed and weak. Riddled with shame. Bound by it.

Several years after I had been caught with the books, I am riding in the car with my mom's boyfriend. He's there to keep me safe as I drive to California to be a youth pastor for a summer. I've been through two years of prayers at my college, where friends watch Jesus heal me. Some of the shame loses its grip.

I sing God's worth to crowds at Maranatha Coffeehouse. My mom and her boyfriend attended one of my performances, which is now the subject of our car conversation. "Your mom was really hurt when you sang," he tells me.

"Why?" Familiar shame roils my stomach.

"You shared in front of everybody that you had a difficult childhood. Imagine how she felt sitting there, hearing those words."

I search my brain. What did I say? Did I share any details? Point the finger? No. As I peel back the memory, I remember saying I had a hard childhood, but that Jesus healed it all. I do not point a finger of condemnation at my mom; I herald Jesus as the hero of my story.

I cower in the seat. Sputter all sorts of I'm-sorrys. Feel plain awful.

But in the recollection, I realize something afresh. My mom took my statement into her heart as accusation, something never intended. I have a world-rocking revelation: perhaps my mom shames because she was shamed. I've heard the mantra before: hurt people hurt people. Perhaps this is the same equation: shamed people shame people.

So I pray for my mom. She does what she knows and she needs to be free of shame too. Not guilt—we all need to realize our guilt so we can run to a loving God to save us—but shame. The Scripture says Jesus despised the shame of the cross. I still don't quite know what that means, but I'm learning.

As I discover my children's warts and dark spots, I fervently pray I don't pass on shame-DNA. It's my tendency too. In a way I feel like Mother Teresa who in her dark journals says she can't see God's love or feel it or touch it. Shame mongering is a lifelong struggle for me, deeply woven into my fiber so tight, God has to unravel me to free me of it. I am not fully free of it today. One of my longings for heaven has to do with being released from shame's tendrils.

I read this verse, praying it's true: "Fear not, for you will not be put to shame; and do not feel humiliated, for you will not be disgraced; but you will forget the shame of your youth" (Isaiah 54:4 NASB).

A recent poem personifies shame as the Wicked Witch of the West:

Berated
She lives inside me
The Wicked Witch of the West
Not the one in Wicked
Who's apparently good
No, not her
The Dorothy one who cackles at Toto
And envies vermilion shoes
It's her, green-faced in wrath
Relentless in pursuit
Up to no good
It'll take a tornado of freedom
To whirl her far away
But the tornado
Never comes near
It's far too busy in Kansas, I hear
So I'm left with her
Cackling in my ear
Telling me my worthlessness
My idiotic ways
Reminding me of failures
That weren't even so
Churning my peace into worry
My joy into fretting
Because, you see
You can't ever please her
She's quick to let you know that

Still, I keep her like a pet
Inside my word-weary soul
Because she says "My Pretty"
And I believe her
For a moment

She's been my companion these many years, the Wicked Witch of Shame. I can taste her shame poison still gurgling in the cauldron I've supplied her. I dance with her when I do something awful, and I eat her shiny apple. I'm learning to let her screech away, learning to say no to her potions. Could it be that my own shameful actions are a thin place, where I'm forced to dethrone the witch? Why does it feel right to keep her close by? Why does enduring her punishments feel holy?

I resonate with the old movie *The Mission* where Robert DeNiro's character drags an impossible weight of junkyard metal up an imposing hill in penance for his sins. Someone cuts his rope and lets the burden tumble recklessly down the mountain.

Shame is my burden. I'm sure Jesus has cut my rope, but I keep tying it back together. I relive my former addiction to pornography, and triple-tie the knot. I second-guess the choices I make even today as my children leave for school. I should have kissed them. Should have prayed more. Should have listened better. I tie knots until the rope holding my shame is one big impossible tangle, while the witch cackles.

Through the knots and the cackling, a still small voice beckons me away to another thin place:

Come away
And meet the real Me
Not the one you've
Made Me to be

The One
Who took the shame
Untied the knots
With my once-is-enough sacrifice
To set you free
Once-for-all
My voice isn't
What you think it is
But you've made it so
Thinking me a harsh deity
Like an angry Hindu god
Bent on destroying
Every little sin
Every little piece of you
You forget
That I
Carried it all
Shed my blood
And said It Is Finished
Can you let it be
Finished?
Or will you spend your life
Atoning your Eve-bent ways?
Let it be
Let it lie
Let it go
And let Me peel away the shame
Memory
By
Memory

17

Reactionary

Reactionary

I freak out.

That's me.

Once a dear counselor friend of mine calls me reactionary, which of course, I react against — strongly.

In high school, I suffer from numerous nosebleeds, the gushing kind that spontaneously erupt during class. During my nosebleed era, I fret about grades far too much. I project my perfectionism onto my unsuspecting mother. When I get a B on a test, I burst into tears. I know I'm overreacting, but I can't seem to help myself. I need the empathy of others more than I need truth. So I blame my mom, say she'll be terribly disappointed in me if I bring home this grade, when, really, she often helps me be less hard on myself. But the ruse works. Friends flock and reassure — all because of my reaction.

Later, I totally freak out when I venture downtown with a group of friends to dance at a teen nightclub. We rent a hotel room to crash in later. While at the dance club, our group dances, shoes to sticky floor, inhaling the secondhand smoke of clove cigarettes. The music is loud, the dance floors full. In the cacophony of punk and New Wave music, a group of three college guys approach our threesome. "Hey, want to come to a great party?" one of them asks. He has perfect teeth.

My best friend says, "Yeah, that sounds great!"

My other friend jumps at the chance.

We three step outside where the night chills my bare arms. I shiver, but not from the bite in the air. I know it is a bad idea to venture to another place with guys older and wiser than we are.

I pull my friends aside. "I don't think this is a good idea."

"Mary, you need to lighten up. It'll be fine," one friend tells me.

I grab my other friend who is bent on going. "You don't know these guys. It's not a good idea."

"Look how they're dressed," she says. "They're preppy — harmless."

I cry. Don't these girls know about men? What they want? What they'll take? I know going with these guys is the wrong choice, but these girls are my ride to our hotel room. I am stuck. And shocked into fear.

The guys pull up in their flashy car, beckoning my friends to follow. By now my two friends are smiling and waving from their car, inviting me to join them. I don't. I pray that somehow I can get to the hotel room or home.

Salvation comes in the form of athletic girls. They're going to the same hotel and are upset they can't go along to the party. They have a tournament the next day and need to get some sleep. I ask for a ride. I cram myself into an already-packed car. As the college guys pull away and my friends follow — honking, laughing, and waving — I say a prayer for their safety. But no matter how much I pray, I feel sick inside — that gut feeling that something terrible will happen.

I pace the hotel room in front of the plate glass window,

looking for signs of my friends. I cry. I worry. I pray. I fret. At 1 a.m., I wonder if I should call their parents? Two a.m. Should I call the police? Three a.m. What can I do? Four a.m. sloths by as I reach the panic stage, weeping uncontrollably. At 4:30 a.m., I see my two friends walk into the hotel below.

"Where have you been?" I scream. Before one friend answers, my voice shrills, "Do you know how worried I've been?" I'm their mother now, laying into delinquent kids coming in way after curfew.

"I don't want to talk about it," one says. The other nods. They drop into bed, clothes still on, and fall asleep, while I pace the room, trying to calm myself enough to follow.

Months later, one pulls me aside. "You want to know what happened that night? Raped," she tells me.

I see how my reactionary ways are sometimes manipulative, sometimes necessary, sometimes out of context. But all of my reactions reveal my own issues. My warped need for a yellow-dressed doll as a sign of love. My addiction to human empathy. My deep fear of men and their predatory ways.

I react again and again, not stopping to think about the ramifications or what issues lie beneath. The older I get, the longer between my over-the-top reactions, but even so, I know a volcano boils deep inside. It's like I develop a better ability to handle life's stress and pressure. I go longer and longer before erupting. But I still erupt. And once I do, I can't control myself.

It happens regularly:

I am listening to a man in ministry talk on and on about church, how the poor church needs parachurch ministry to help it along. He's been dissing the church for a year now, and these latest words ignite my volcano. "Stop it," I say. "You will not talk about the church that way." Everyone in the room rubbernecks their gazes to me, stunned. Mild-mannered Mary has had enough, and spews her anger.

I am sitting in a ministry meeting when a woman attacks my friend with verbal daggers. She's been doing it far too long. I shake my head and firmly say, "You will not talk to my friend that way." More rubbernecking because I've raised my voice.

I am in France and our landlord tries to swindle more money from us. I shake my head and leave the room, muttering, "I need to leave or I'm going to start swearing." (This is one of those instances my children remind me of by saying things like, "Mom, remember when you had to go outside because you wanted to swear at the landlord?")

I am on the phone, and the person on the other line makes fun of me and calls me selfish for the umpteenth time. I hang up and fling the phone across the room. I can't seem to keep that volcano down, where the lava flows like a river in springtime.

I discover I have been betrayed by a friend, and I melt into gut-heaving sobs — the kind that sound inconsolable.

I ache. I hurt. I worry. I fear. And I react. Sometimes strongly. Something inside me needs taming. Could it be that my overreaction is a thin place where I can meet God? How can my issues be that sort of meeting place?

Maybe in those moments of emotion something deeper is at play. I'm reacting against my lack of control, my inability to get what I want or to change the outcome of a situation. It's like a great yawp coming from the lava within me that exclaims, "I am not in control, and I don't like it!"

Like a freaky scene from the documentary *Beyond and Back*

that chronicles the "lives" of folks after they die but regain consciousness, I try to see myself from God's perspective, from His bird's-eye view of things. I hover over myself, watch myself rail against my lack of control. I see me cry. I see me throw the phone. I see me crumple in upon myself, grief stricken. And, though it's hard, I fight to have compassion for me.

Funny how I can watch another person fall apart and long to come to her side in empathy, but when I see me do the same things, a strange coldness takes over. I tell myself, "Get over it. Don't react so much. Don't feel. Don't go there. Buck up. Come on now. Get ahold of yourself for crying out loud."

Recently, I break down weeping in the café at church. My husband and I have navigated a rough year in the aftermath of church planting in France. We are talking about it, mining the pain. The weight of all those trials hits while a song with the words, "It's all for You; I'm letting go" plays from the monitors above us. It's the worship song that stuns me earlier, and its message is playing havoc with my emotions.

People drink coffee. They have conversations.

And I weep. Hands over my face. Breathing in the grief of our time in France, exhaling the pain, hoping that if I exhale enough it will fly through the café ceiling, to the heavens and never, ever come back.

Patrick looks at me, bewildered. He looks around. "Pull yourself together," he tells me. He does not wear grief the way I do. He analyzes it well. I emote it.

My critical voice berates me for the reaction. I sniff in my tears, shake my head, look around to see if anyone in the emptying café notices. If they have, they've blessedly looked away.

"I'm going to get the kids," he tells me.

I am alone at the table, wet faced. I gather myself, sneak down a back hallway, eyes to the ground, and pull myself together in our minivan, sunglasses hiding red eyes.

I breathe in. I breathe out. I pray. I try to relinquish control, like the song says. My life is all for Jesus, at least I want it to be. And that control I think I want and need? I'm letting it go. I can't control life's sticky outcomes. I can't create good memories where none exist. It's not an easy thing for me, as control—keeping the volcano under wraps—is my safe place. When my world is molten in chaos, control is where I flee. When my issues rise higher and more deadly than Mount St. Helens, pulling my life back into manageable proportions is my fallback plan. But even control is illusionary. And, frail as I am, I can't maintain it for long anyway.

It's all for You.

It's all for You.

I'm letting go.

I'm letting go.

And maybe some of that letting go means getting rid of that critical voice inside me, believing better of me than worse. To playfully accept that I react, that I am awash in issues, that I'm feeble at holiness. That I need God's grace terribly. That I don't always grieve in a way that makes others comfortable.

I'm watching again that little blonde-headed girl. She's running down store aisles, looking behind her, clutching a boxed doll to her chest like treasure.

The recollection can either be a thin place or a shame place. I take a breath. Breathe in and then out. I breathe in God's grace for me; I exhale the shame. I cling to Jesus and let go of my control.

In the center of the store, the manager turns. He sees the little girl, drops the merchandise he's inventorying, and runs to her, arms outstretched. "You're found! You're found," he says. He kneels. His eyes become God's eyes—full of compassion, over brimming with the kind of empathy the girl's been longing for, the kind of love the girl thinks money can buy, but can't.

"Silly you," he cajoles. "The doll won't fill you up. You've been chasing after dust, crying like a banshee for something I'd willingly give you all along." He holds the little girl, as she drops the doll to the linoleum floor.

It's all for You.

I'm letting go.

18

Conan

She sits near me, eyes wet, realizing all at once that her daddy never really approved. She says she jumped through every hoop, but he didn't notice. Years and years later, she weeps at the recollection of never, ever being enough. Enough to love. As she does every sort of perfection acrobatics, her sister walks a different path. And Daddy overlooks my friend, gazes beyond all her hard work to be approved, and lavishes love on the sister that never sought it. Bitter, cleansing tears come in the realization, accompanied by a quiver of hope in her voice.

I cry too.

I understand.

Ten hours later I sit on the couch, sandwiched between my daughters. We watch a film about an addled man befriending and blessing an entire town with his simplicity and forgiveness. The three of us weep. Not the trickle of tears running down cheeks, but diaphragm heaving sobs as we suck in tears. We are moved because the character loves so freely. He just loves. And folks don't always get it.

I get it.

Or at least I think I do.

I want that kind of love.

I need it.

My daughter Julia sniffles again after the movie, her blonde head resting on my shoulder. "He reminds me of Jesus," Julia says, "the way he takes everyone's blame." Falling apart in my arms, she has a personal revival while I stroke her hair. And I dream of love sacrificial.

Julia's words bring Conan to mind. Horn-rimmed glasses as thick as the width of a number two pencil, hair greasy from neglect, jeans too small or too big—the product of a grand-mother who doesn't know fashion. Conan just loves folks. He is in my French class. He puts on plays for us, in French of course. He makes us laugh. His eccentricity and tenacity worm their way into our hearts. And into my mom's heart.

She buys him a bike.

She worries about him.

I am happy she does.

Really.

But in the recollection, I coach myself. "Be happy, Mary. Remember Conan with joy. See your mom's affection for him as a testament to the love inside her. Don't feel what you're trying to stuff down. Don't go there."

But I'm in my forties now, and I'm learning it's healthier to go there. So I do.

I am jealous of Conan, who doesn't try to earn my mom's love but gets it freely anyway. I'm like my friend, upset that I jump through hoops, believing if I get it right, do the correct things, act the appropriate way, that I'll merit her affection. But it seldom works the way I envision it. And all that effort makes me tired.

Since my father left the earth, thirty years ago now, I fear I place a larger premium on my mother's approval and love. Maybe it's too much pressure. Maybe I ask more than I should. And maybe all my longing is displaced.

I see Conan, his simple ways, and I see Jesus. I've made my life too complicated, so unlike the child Jesus asks me to be. It's really quite simple. Despite others' failings, despite my daddy-shaped hole, despite my own gnawing need, Jesus stands before me, arms spread wide as a cornfield, beckoning me to belong to Him. His embrace is not fickle. It doesn't fly away like chaff on the wind. It's not dependent upon me running-running-running on the hamster wheel of perfectionism, hoping for approval.

When a famous ministry leader comes to our church and wows us all with a stirring message, I decide to meet him. But he's like the president of evangelicalism, so I'm full of anxiety. I hope my pastor standing near him will introduce us, will let him know I'm not a nobody, that I write books. All this rushes through my head as I enter the greeting area.

I scold myself for wanting to be recognized.

I nearly turn on my heels and run from the reception line, but something holds me there. Is it a need to be seen? To shake the hand of a "famous" person? Probably a combination of all that, to tell the truth.

As it nears my turn, I fret. What will I say? What can I say? I fiddle with my hands, standing off to the side while the ministry leader laughs and engages with the person in front of me.

In a moment, it's my turn. I push my hand forward, but as I do, another hand darts in from the side. He shakes the other hand, his eyes half on me, half on the other person. His gaze is saying, "I'm busy here, can't you see?" My pastor has left by this point, so there will be no special introduction.

I have one quick moment. "I was blessed by your message," I say.

"Thanks." He nods, then turns his full attention to the other person.

I walk away, wondering why I want to cry. I'm shaking inside. Something about the meeting burns inside me. It's certainly not the leader's fault. The situation is a picture of how I feel most of my childhood.

In the way.

A mistake.

A pesky interruption.

Someone who stands off to the side, longing to be noticed, but learning to pretend happiness when I'm overlooked.

A girl who has to prove her worth, but never quite does.

And all I really want is Conan love. Unconditional affection.

Once my friend Julie says, "Mary, I notice that you're always busy. Like when something's cooking in the microwave, you're wiping the counters, loading the dishwasher. I admire that. I do that now too."

I smile when Julie tells me that. It's always nice to hear you've rubbed off on someone in a positive way. But I am not so sure I'm happy with her words. She means them kindly, but they echo in my head like truth. I cannot stop. I must always work. I must always prove that I am worthy to take up space on this earth. Like my friend at the beginning of the chapter, I run ragged trying to please a fickle audience. Meanwhile, Jesus opens His arms wide to me. But I'm too crushed by my own unworthiness to see His welcome.

I paint a new picture of the famous ministry leader encounter. The man looks my way. I'm shyly standing in the corner. He moves toward me, only he wears the face of Conan. Then Jesus.

His smile is broad. I turn away. Why would He want to see me? I haven't produced enough to merit his attention. Others shove hands into His while I shrink mine away and look at the ground, recounting my worthlessness.

Like the Prodigal's father, He flat out runs to me in front of everyone, twirls me in His arms like a father would, and whispers, "I love you, Mary. Just for you. Rest now. Stop your hurrying and racing and proving. I'm not the father who died. I'm not the mother who didn't notice. I'm the One who loves you enough to run across a room."

I need that Jesus. My friend who weeps over her father's fickle affections needs that Jesus. The Jesus who runs when we're too tired to run anymore. The Jesus who is bigger than our mommies and daddies, whose love triumphs over our deepest, quietest sins. Who loves us when we're raggedy and unlovable. Who holds us when we feel we don't have reason to occupy earth. Who notices when others don't.

Can I just say it out loud right here? I love Jesus.

And little by little, I'm learning He loves me. And He's using my emptiness, my longing for parents who would love me for me, my jealousy of my mother's kind affection for Conan—all of this He uses as a thin place to show me that human love is beautifully fragile, but His is perfect, even when I'm not.

19

Bob

I joke as a junior in high school that I will have a boyfriend named Bob. I become so obsessed with all things boyfriend that I can't seem to think of anything else. At night, I wallow over the sad fact that I never get asked to a homecoming dance, that I'm unworthy of male attention. I pray like a crazy woman, prayers like, "Jesus, if You really love me, You'll send me a boyfriend. Now. You know I want one. Why won't You give me one?" My journals of that time typify my anguish:

I seesaw between despair over God's complete disinterest in my dating life and hope that maybe He's preparing just the right Bob for me.

Then one day it happens. My wildly worldly friend Jessica flits into Biology, smiling. "You'll just never guess," she says.

"What?"

"I found him."

"Who?" I ask.

"Bob the Boyfriend! I've located him for you."

"Really?"

"Yeah! He's tallish, really nice, and he's one of those funda-mentalist Christians who's always spouting off Bible verses. I told him all about you, and here's the kicker." She pauses for dramatic effect. "He's going to call you and ask you out on a date!"

Funny thing—I'm thrilled. I can't help but smile. God has answered my long-asked-for prayer.

"But there's one more thing. His name really is Bob!"

That's when I laugh with joy. God surely has answered my prayer.

That evening Bob the Boyfriend calls me. We agree to meet at the only place he knows about in my suburb: a computer repair place. (I should've taken this as a sign.)

When we meet it's pretty darned awkward. He's not the dashing Bob I imagine in my dreams. I surmise that Jessica catches wind of Bob's name and his penchant for all things evangelical and overlooks Bob's exterior: awkward, pimply, bespectacled. But it's not his looks that take me aback; it's his demeanor—overeager and seemingly uptight. I suck in a breath, tell him I'm happy to meet him. When he opens the car door for me, a long-stemmed red rose sits on the seat. Inwardly, I groan, but I say thank you.

Bob takes me bowling. He has a coupon for it, he says. "Do you like nuts?" he asks, halfway through frame four.

"Um, yeah, I do."

He pulls out another coupon. "We'll go to the mall and get these nuts at the House of Nuts, okay?"

After the nut excursion, he tells me about a park where we can feed the ducks. "This is where me and my buddies go swimming," he tells me. All I can see is the duck doo slicking the muddy shores. "Come on, let's go wading." He takes off his shoes.

"No thanks," I say.

But he persists. "Oh, it'll be fun. We can walk along the shore of the lake."

"I'm really not up to it."

On the way back to the computer repair shop rendezvous point, I feel stupid. All that pining for Bob the Boyfriend has crashed into reality. Has God played a strange joke on me?

"Mary, I need to know one thing: what is your spiritual gift?" Bob says as we near the computer store.

I look at him. I'm a fairly new Christian, not knowing at all what he means. "Um, I like to sing?"

He shakes his head. "I'll have to teach you about that," he says.

We say goodbye and I drive away a little wiser, a lot more cautious about what I pray for.

But even after bowling with Bob, I pine for a boyfriend. I ache for one like a thirsty dog pants for water. It's obsessive.

Hunting for "Bob" populates nearly every page of my high school and college journals. He's on every prayer request list I write. I pray about Bob, for Bob. Every single man I meet I size up for boyfriend potential. I have a thousand crushes, most leading nowhere. Bob is everywhere, but he doesn't seem to notice me.

While this wreaks havoc on my self-esteem, I see now how God's firm answer of no is the most beautiful thin place of my life. In those times of wrestling with Him over His debilitating no, I see how very much I need Him, and how quickly He'd be replaced by Bob. And if I tell myself the truth, I know way down deep that I will place Bob on the throne of my life. Couple that with the rape at five and my gaping need for a father, I see God's severe mercy on my life during those years. So many with similar upbringings walk a painful path of sexual impurity. If I look myself in the mirror, I see my own potential to sin.

My journals chronicle my yearning for all things Bob-ish:

"I like this guy, a junior, named Jay. The only thing I can say is that I am going to pray that he is a Christian, or that God will show me a Christian boy soon! It's so hard to be patient. Now, since this will probably come to nothing, I will try not to get my hopes up. I'll be open to God's suggestions as He makes them clear to me."

"Then came the issue of the loneliness and the boyfriend void I seem to always have in my life. I stopped asking guys to dance — I ended up either dancing with the few boys who asked me (no slow songs) or by myself."

"Someone is going to ask me to Homecoming. Everyone knows who except me — and they won't tell me. So now I expect it, and if it doesn't happen I will be more crushed than I ever have been in my entire life. I hope they are not pulling a prank on me by saying this."

"The Lord is saving someone for me. Sometimes He has to yell that to me, but deep down I always know that. It's hard sometimes."

"Life is so unfair. I'm not a bad person. I'm not ugly, but oh yes, I don't have a date for Homecoming, of course. A lot of girls aren't going so it's not that bad. But I haven't been on a date for a year and a half, and I wouldn't even consider that a date at all. What's the use? I don't understand. I seem like a nice person. I wish someone would just hold me and say, 'Everything's going to be okay.' But no one will. All the men in my life are gone. They all left me. I'm just alone when it comes to guys. I guess marriage is out of the picture. I've been raped, gone through divorce, had my dad die, moved several times, and suffered a lot, but no I guess I don't deserve to go out. I'm unclean. Won't anyone understand me? I hate this world. I hate it. I hate it. I hate it. I can't understand why I've had such a crummy life and I don't get any guys. What am I? An ugly duckling? If You're trying to humble me, God, congratulations, You did it. I am now a human with no purpose. I know I am to be truly satisfied with You. But I have human needs too. I need to be held."

"I was thinking about boys today and the Lord put this thought into my head: When you are looking for a penny, you seldom find it. But when you aren't looking for one, when you least expect it, there it will be shining in the sunlight. It is a pleasant surprise, not a conquest or something to be sought after. The Lord will provide in a pleasant, surprising, exciting way. It's the same with relationships. If I sought after one, it would not be a pleasant surprise, but a somewhat expected relationship. I wouldn't be grateful to God for it."

"Yesterday a guy called me by accident. He was so cool—a total Christian. It was so neat hearing from him. Maybe just maybe the Lord has something in mind. I will pray for His will. I wrote him a letter of encouragement. He leads a prayer group at school and was on the 700 Club! I've only talked to him ten minutes."

I ache for me back then, how tethered I am to male attention. And really, it all falls back on my desire to be held and comforted as a parent would comfort. I placed on men the insufferable burden of becoming my parents—shoes no man should fill.

Even though I plead and cry and hope, God, in His sovereign kindness, holds all the Bobs far, far away for a long, long time. In college when I meet a man who I nearly place on the throne, God graciously severs the relationship, leaving me licking my wounds and asking all sorts of whys. For two years, I flounder in bewilderment, only to realize, finally, that I don't want to live my life for any Bob. I want to live for Jesus.

I walk down the wedding aisle wearing white. By God's grace, I stay pure for my husband-to-be. Though I know I am spoiled by those boys so many years ago, at least when I have a choice in the matter, I say a firm no, preferring purity to sexual sin. I'm somewhat of an anomaly at the junior high where I teach when it slips out that I'm a virgin when I marry. Right before the wedding, a fourteen-year-old girl pulls me aside and whispers, "Don't worry, okay? It hurts at first, but it gets better."

God painstakingly prepares me for Patrick, not Bob. He shows me the important truth that no one man can fill all the empty, gaping places of my heart. I carry this lesson into marriage, learning afresh that Patrick is a great husband, but he is not Jesus. Truth be told, I'm happiest in my marriage when I run to Jesus first.

I'm happiest in life too.

20

Material Girl

I don't realize it's stealing until my father's second wife brings back the memory. "It did bother me when you and your father went shopping in the basement of his house." She uses her fingers to make air quotes around shopping—and all at once I realize I spent much of my childhood as a thief.

Jim's adventures in Eleanor's basement starts my life as a material girl—longing for things that aren't mine to have. Or wanting things so much that I'm willing to criminalize myself. I look for my hidden Christmas gifts, snoop for their hiding places. Though I don't resort to a life of petty crime, I am guilty of pining whine—a trait so intrinsic to me that I don't know when I'm doing it. I pine. I whine. And I toss contentment to the breeze.

My closet in ninth grade attests to this. My room has a tiny closet tucked under the stairs, nary enough space to hold a few hanging items. But upstairs in our unfinished attic, a closet stretches several linear feet. That's where my clothes live and breathe and boast their trendiness. I have old clothes in there that don't fit me anymore. I hang hand-me-downs there too, along with clothes my grandmother makes me. I don't wear all those clothes, but I need to feel I have a lot. And when I visit my friends' homes, I pine after their closets too, even if my friends have less than me.

I compare homes too. All growing up, I feel less than others. Instead of contentment, I pine for others' things. I lament our floral couch, how out of style it is—a clear violation of my fashion boundaries. When we get a beige sectional, I nearly cry with joy.

In college, I apply for a summer job at a photography studio. I walk into the fluorescent-lit "studio," eyes squinting. It's sandwiched between several other industrial buildings—architecture meets Costco box. The hum of the overhead lights irritate me.

"You're here for the job, right?" An overmakeupped lady shoves a clipboard into my hand. "Here's the application."

She takes me into the back room behind the studio. In the hallway, cheesy-looking adults and kids smile back at me from particleboard frames.

"Here's your script." She hands me a typed piece of paper. "After a few calls, you'll have it memorized."

I sit at a long table. Three others nod at me. A tired-looking balding man, pen behind his ear. A girl whose night job might be of ill repute. An overweight curly-headed girl who turned away from me, as if she were afraid I would copy her sales secrets. In the center of the table sits a rickety, three-legged barbecue.

A phone book page stares back at me, launching my one-day career as a telemarketer. "Hello, I'm Mary from New World Photography. How'd you like to win a free barbecue grill?" Click.

"If you'd just answer these three questions, you could win." Click.

"Who was the first president of the United States?" Click.

I remember the day as if it were captured in a photograph. How the barbecue grill keeps falling over. The drudgery of repeating words. The outlandish answers — Elvis, the first president? The girl who pulls me aside to say I-am-a-Christian-and-I-hate-that-girl-over-there. I decide then, at nineteen, that this is one crazy world we live in, where shoddy barbecues (and overpriced picture packages) are forced upon telemarketing-weary folks over the phone. I hate that I create a need folks don't even have.

It's a lie, you know. That stuff can fill a heart. And yet I believe that lie most of my life. If someone loves me, they'll buy me stuff. It'll fill for a moment, then I'll want more. I'm like Madame Blueberry of Veggie Tales fame, gorging on the aisles of Stuff Mart, but never satisfied. No wonder there are 12-step groups for shopaholics!

We spend two years in France before our family ventures home on furlough. In France we are blessedly free of advertising for the most part. No ads on TV, very few print ads. The only advertisements we see are for perfume or fashion on small billboards as we walk the kids to school or when we drive places. People in France aren't entrenched in stuff; they are much more about lifestyle — spending time with family and friends around a dinner table, being able to truly relax during long stretches of vacation.

We land in Dallas. A friend picks us up and drives us the hour stretch home. Lining the freeway are stores of every ilk.

"Look, there's Target," says one kid.

"Oh, Walmart," exclaims another.

"Ooooh, T.J. Maxx," squeals the third.

On and on this goes until one of my kids says: "Mattress Giant! Let's go to Mattress Giant."

Patrick and I exchange looks. When have we ever been to that store? In one millisecond, my kids morph from contentment to materialism.

Which goes to show we're all susceptible.

This encounter with Mattress Giant comes on the heels of the greatest financial curse and blessing of my life. Before we move to France, we sell our home to a man from our church. A girl in a prayer meeting tells me about him. She hands me his card. "He can help you," she tells me. So we check him out, and everything seems hunky dory. We sign papers and fly to France to be church planters, believing our house is blessedly sold.

Four months later, a few weeks before Christmas, our bank calls. "Why aren't you making your mortgage payments?" the nice lady asks.

"Um, because we sold our house," I reply.

"No you didn't."

Those words start a flurry of investigation. Turns out the man we "sold" our home to is a con artist. He creates paperwork that shows he owns the title of our home, but unbeknownst to us, we still own the loan. He is squatting in our home, destroying it. Friends drive by and take pictures. The carpet is horribly soiled by a dog allowed free reign inside. The garden, destroyed. Cabinets broken. Even if we want to catch up on the mortgage, we can't, since he still owns the title. Foreclosure is our only option, and we are forced to take it.

I rant and cry and growl. I shake my fist at the heavens, wondering why God allows this to happen. After all, we're missionaries! For two weeks, I stalk around our rented French home in bewilderment. I whine to God: "But Lord, we followed all the correct paths. And in one instant, all that means nothing? Our perfect credit violated because of the misdeeds of a con artist?"

How will we recover?

How could we be so stupid?

Will we lose everything?

It feels as if all my materialistic ways are rolling into one giant ball of razor string. And that string has wrapped itself around and around my soul, terrifying and trapping me.

Imprisoned there, I am asked a question: "Do you really believe I am in control?"

Then another: "Do you really believe I own the cattle on a thousand hills?"

Then another: "Do you really believe I am good?"

Then another: "Do you really believe I am sovereign over this situation?"

Like Job after God vomits His majesty all over him, I suddenly feel small. What I say I believe about God and what I actually believe are two different things. That sad revelation shakes me way down deep. Like the father of the demon-possessed boy in Mark 9:24, I holler, "I do believe; help my unbelief" (NASB).

I do believe He is in control; only I don't live like I do.

I do believe He owns the cattle on a thousand hills, but I doubt He'll give one to me.

I do believe God is good, yet I question His goodness when our house is vandalized and stolen.

I do believe God is sovereign — well, except for in that one spot of real estate where our house languishes in foreclosure. He can't be sovereign there.

Losing the house is like looking into a mirror. I see who I really am — inextricably tied to possessions, defined by them, enslaved by them. I am more interested in financial security than I am in the kingdom of God. And I believe more in the power of the mighty dollar than the beautiful sovereignty of the Mighty God.

Eventually my complaints fade.

In the thin place of financial instability, I find God. I meet Him afresh.

I can't explain it. I wake up one day, free. My life has been one of worry, bound up by money, consumed by managing it correctly. In an instant, God gives me a surprising gift: peace. It's a painful walk through foreclosure, and I prefer not to have to go through it again, yet I believe God uses it in my life. He gives me an astounding gift, infusing in me the belief that He is in control, ruling the world just the way He wants to. I don't need to fret and pine and grab.

One night I have a dream. When I wake up, I write the dream down in story form. It's really the story of God's surprising transformation of me in the midst of our house trial:

> Little Aaron sat in the center of his bedroom floor, holding his knees to his chest, rocking back and forth. He could hear the mayhem in other rooms, something he'd grown accustomed to when Mama announced they were moving.
>
> But today the commotion had nothing to do with movers.
>
> No, it had to do with Miss Mine.
>
> Miss Mine, as Aaron came to call her, crashed into their home early that morning. She noted the boxes nearly stacked to the ceiling with a sneer. Aaron knew Miss Mine was thrilled his family was finally leaving.
>
> "I'm taking what is mine," she said. When Mama stepped aside, letting her into the living room, Aaron's stomach lurched. How could Mama do such a thing? Miss Mine would take everything!
>
> Miss Mine pushed her way through. She glared at Mama. She opened cabinets. "Why'd you pack all your stuff already?" she asked.
>
> "It is ours," Mama said simply.

Miss Mine growled. Hit a wall with her left fist. Aaron watched Miss Mine's blood streak down the perfectly white wall. He didn't dare clean it up until after she left.

"We'll see about 'ours,'" she said. "Where's his stuff?"

Mama hadn't said a thing. Not one single word. This, of course, made Miss Mine's face grow as red as the blood on the walls. "I aim to take everything that's mine, you hear me? Now where is his stuff?"

But Mama kept quiet.

So Miss Mine threw her arms in the air. "I'm taking what's mine." She motioned to the front door. Her family burst through. "Take whatever you can carry."

That's when Aaron went to his room, placed himself in its center, hoping Miss Mine and her relatives would leave him alone. After all, there were no cabinets in his room. Just boxes full of toys and shorts and balls. His own stuff.

But the rummaging made him peek through the doorway. He watched as Miss Mine grabbed things from every cabinet — his cabinets. She took aprons Mama would've looked beautiful in, serving trays made of dark, carved wood, shiny glasses, tablecloths, clocks. She threw everything into large sheets, instructing her family to tie up the ends and haul them outside.

Mama tried to stop her once. "You can't—"

"I can and I will. Who's going to stop me? You?" With that she punched Mama in the cheek, sending her into the wall. Aaron ran to her, stroked her beautiful hair. He stood as tall as he could, facing Miss Mine.

"You will leave our house," he said.

But Miss Mine just cackled. "This stuff is mine. Mine, hear me?"

Aaron sang songs for Mama. "Twinkle, Twinkle, Little Star." "This Little Light of Mine." "The Itsy Bitsy Spider." He put a strong arm around her, trying to protect her, while crashing and thumping and shoving punctuated the house.

"Well, I'm leaving you." Miss Mine spat on the floor before them. "With everything I ever wanted. Thanks for being so accommodating." She turned and walked away.

Aaron counted every step. Seventeen. He heard the front door slam. He ran to it and locked it tight.

Mama appeared like a ghost beside him. She placed a weak arm around his shoulder. "It's time to leave," she said. "The movers will be here any minute."

"But Mama. Miss Mine took our things. Aren't you going to run after her? Or call the police?"

Mama smiled, her swollen face making her lips crooked. Aaron thought she never looked more beautiful. "She didn't take what was ours. She took what is his. The landlord's. I spent every day in this home making sure his things were safe. I took good care of them, dusting and cleaning. I let him know if I accidentally broke something. He responded with grace. Always grace. No," she looked right into Aaron's eyes, "Miss Mine took his things, not ours. And he will exact a fair punishment."

Relief washed over Aaron. He'd forgotten during all the crashing and throwing that it wasn't Mama Miss Mine was taking from, though it sure felt like it. Miss Mine took from the landlord. Poor Miss Mine.

Aaron took Mama's hand. They made a pathway

through the boxes. They stepped into the sunlight of the garden. Aaron knew the same sun shot its laughter on their heads and Miss Mine's head too. Strange, he thought, how the sun made no distinction.

"It's time to move on," Mama said. "To leave this all behind."

Aaron smiled and said, "I'm ready."

Like Aaron, I'm ready. I'm sick of being a material girl, clinging to my possessions as if they are really mine. I'm tired of feeding off Stuff Mart. And when I see God equated to stuff, or preachers promising God's obligation to financially bless His followers (as long as they send in that seed gift of faith), I want to overturn tables. When I walk into the Dollar Store and spy a magnet with cutesy slogans, I roll my eyes:

God is like Coke. He's the real thing.

God is like General Electric. He lights your path.

God is like Bayer Aspirin. He works wonders.

God is like Hallmark cards. He cares enough to send the very best.

God is like Tide. He gets the stains out that others leave behind.

God is like VO5 Hairspray. He holds through all kinds of weather.

God is like Alka Seltzer. Try Him. You'll like Him.

God is like Scotch Tape. You can't see Him, but you know He's there.

God is not reduced to slogans. He is not boxed in by marketing gimmicks. He loves us, yes. In fact He loves me so much, He gives me the gift of foreclosure so I can realize how much better He is than things. He loves me enough to slay the insidious idolatry in my heart. The apostle Paul says it well: "Don't be greedy, for a greedy person is an idolater" (Colossians 3:5 NLT). Before, I used to think that if God truly loved me, He'd give me everything I want, not realizing that getting everything I want will give me an idolatrous heart. And a meaningless life: "Enjoy what you have," Solomon says, "rather than desiring what you don't have. Just dreaming about nice things is meaningless — like chasing the wind" (Ecclesiastes 6:9 NLT).

When the con man stole our house, I bet he didn't know he was doing me a spiritual favor. Through that trial, a piece of my idolatry is severed, and my pursuit of stuff severely squelched. I'm no longer the little girl stealing treasures from Eleanor. I'm not the teenager who needs a full closet. I'm not a part of the consumer machine, selling photo packages no one needs. And I'm not the woman who is defined by perfect credit. I'm just a girl, holding Jesus' hand, learning to trust Him, believing that holding His hand is better than anything else this life has to offer. "I have God's more-than-enough, more joy in one ordinary day than they get in all their shopping sprees. At day's end I'm ready for sound sleep, for You, God, have put my life back together" (Psalm 4:7 – 8 MSG).

21

Signs

When I meet Jesus, I start chasing signs. I crave knowing God is around every corner, infusing every circumstance. I read newsletters from David Wilkerson that detail his own adventure with chasing after signs. Particularly once I finish *The Cross and the Switchblade*, I believe God will make His way known, that He will directly guide me in every endeavor.

In my late teens, I venture outside, past a long dirt road, and come upon a clearing. There's a stash of moldy books splayed open to the sky, scattering the ground like casualties. I read each opened page, searching for a word from God. Surely, He meant for me to come across these books, these words. But the engineering texts say very little to me.

In college, I become hyper-aware of Jesus. And Satan too. How they're battling for the souls of fellow students. I meet friends who pray for revival, who seem to have a word from God as often as pickled beets appear on the salad bar. So I hang with them, glean from them, hoping God will give me signs.

As a group, we drive to my friend's parents' home several weekends, hoping to refuel so we can do battle on our campus. Though excited, I shudder inside. The mom is a spiritually powerful woman, the kind who makes me want to cower in a corner unnoticed, hiding from an embarrassing word from God she might say about me in front of everyone. She says such words at whim, while she's cooking stevia-sweetened brownies, straightening her home, or watching football. It's impossible to predict when God will burst forth.

She prays for me. Internally, I resist. Though my friends are splayed on the floor like flopped-over dominoes, reveling in some unknown bliss, I plant my feet and stay standing. She asks God to please give me the gift of tongues, but I keep my mouth shut. I leave with a vague sense of failure. Though I resist her advances, I sense a subtle pressure to give in. I wonder if I'm quenching the Spirit.

My church is of the charismatic persuasion too. College retreats find me planting my feet, fearful inside of letting go, all the while worrying that I'm an ingrate toward the Spirit. Still, through it all, I pray. I ask Jesus to be real, to give me a sign He's near, in a way that I know He's real. I don't want to receive some amazing gift in the heat of emotionalism. But even as I pray this I worry that I'm trying to orchestrate God.

Healers come through my church. They anoint me with oil. Some folks talk about how our backs are misaligned, that if I put my legs directly in front of me, I'll see how poorly aligned I am. When I do so, and I see the misalignment, they pray for me, pulling my shorter leg as they pray. "It's a miracle," one says, as my leg apparently "grows" with their pull. I smile, but worry. I distinctly felt the person physically make my feet align.

Another couple tells how they sell everything, buy a Winnebago, and then ask God for a sign as to where they should go next. "Did you know the word Phoenix is in the Bible?" they ask a waiting congregation. "Well, it is, and we're going there." So they leave on their journey to faraway Phoenix, but return home soon after.

A Holy Spirit car wash nearly flattens me. A group of people stands across from each other. If they join hands at the top, they all look like London Bridge Is Falling Down, only the tunnel they make is a good fifteen people deep. I step a toe into the car wash. The first two people lay hands on me and pray, then the next, then the next, until I'm on my knees by person fifteen. I claim it as a healing victory, a sign from God that He sees me and loves me.

And, really, these folks usher in the most significant healing in my life. They believe God will come near, pour His presence out upon my fragile soul, and change me. Because of their consistent prayers, I am who I am today. Not perfect, but whole.

During this time, in the midst of all this praying and searching for signs, an interesting thing happens. My roommate leaves one evening, giving me free reign of our dorm room. I slip onto the floor, my knees hitting our brought-in carpet (otherwise they'd hit cold linoleum). I pray for Jesus to please come near. I tell Him I love Him. I say I want to follow Him forever. Then I'm silent. I try to pray again, but my words jumble in my mouth. Soon, another language flows out from me, a simple gift in the quiet of my room. No hype. No pushing me over. No songs or crying or Holy Spirit car washes. I love that God so deeply knows my heart that He gifts me with this in the silence of my room.

Electricity shoots from me when I pray for my friend in California, the summer of my junior year of college. She's having abdominal issues and when I place my hand there, something zings through me. Neither of us speaks about it for a long time. I've never experienced zinging prayers since.

When I go to Malaysia after college, I'm surrounded by folks needing signs. The pastor tells me he believes I am being called to stay indefinitely. Others come alongside in agreement. I waffle back and forth, even have a vision or two, but in the end, I decide to get a job back in the United States, though the signs point elsewhere.

I see the necessity of signs when we begin our walk with Jesus, just as a baby needs the cocooning presence of parents who love her. But as we grow, we stretch our wills. We don't always need our parents' nearness. And, actually, it's a sign of maturity that we trust our parents' love though they may not constantly demonstrate care.

I believe He sends signs—just as He was kind to wet and blow-dry the fleece for doubting Gideon. I believe God performs miracles. I believe He is bigger than our perception of Him. But I also know He's a loving Father who doesn't spoil His children. Sometimes He's necessarily near. To teach us faith, sometimes He's far. Sometimes He allows bad things to happen, all sifted through His sovereign hands. I don't really like that part, but it's not up to me. God is the epitome of mystery and cannot be manipulated or managed, though I try my darnedest to do both.

It's what I love about God—He's that wild Aslan lion, good but not safe. The God who lights the minutiae on our path one moment and sends us darkness the next. Signs and their lack are both thin places, one to confirm Himself, the other to confirm our faith. Most days I want it all spelled out; but if I live life that way, I will never grow.

I liken it to Job, who begins his godly life with blessings aplenty —God's signs like bless-me billboards on his life. God seems to abandon the manner He deals with Job, not only removing blessings, but also removing signs of Himself. In angst, Job questions, wrestles, then questions some more. Eventually, God lambastes him with questions Job cannot answer, showing him God is God and Job is not. The result is Job's repentance. And a startling revelation:

"I have heard of You by the hearing of the ear," Job says to God. "But now my eye sees You" (Job 42:5 NASB). God's very scarcity is the thin place Job dances on, from hearing God to seeing Him. I'm sure he doesn't much like all the abandonment, deaths, and trials. He lives bewildered in the wilderness God places him in. But somehow in the darkness, where no signs come, Job sees God. Really sees Him.

Long ago, Jesus walks the paths we walk. He experiences the deep presence of His Father for many years — along with confirming signs and wonders and awe. But in one heart-ripping moment, Jesus feels God's absence like we'll never feel — the utter void of the goodness of God the Father as He turns His back on His Son. Complete abandonment. Silence from the heavens. Darkness shrouding signs. Then death. After three days of eternity, resurrection.

It's that way in my life too. Early on: signs. Later in my walk with Jesus: darkness. The result after the darkness: an oxymoronic closeness to God — my own resurrection from the darkness.

Today I don't ask for signs as a prerequisite for me to follow God. I don't often seek fleeces before I step out. That's not to say signs won't come; they may. But in looking back upon the wildernesses God has helped me stumble through, I am thankful. God gives signs. He takes them away.

As Job says, "Blessed be Your name," either way.

22

Children

My mom misses me when I go away to college. She sends me notes, encourages me, tells me she loves me. She sends me care packages. As I grow into adulthood, my mom grows in her tenderness toward me. In my journal, I write, "I talked to Mom about her being alone and she said it wasn't as hard as she thought it would be. I felt an underlying loneliness in her. I did feel she was being honest. It was just a segment of a fragmented conversation, but I'm glad it came out."

Later, I write, "Yesterday my mom sent me a really neat letter: 'I really enjoyed your homecoming thanksgiving. We had nice times together. It's fun to sit on the couch and gab a lot, isn't it? I want you to know how special you are to me. You are!' I cried."

Ours is a relationship of undulation. Pain, forgiveness, misunderstanding—all flow together to create a complicated fountain. I spring from her. She springs from me. And sometimes the water runs dry. And so often I'm thirsty.

But I want to be a mommy whose love flows freely into her children. The day I become a mother, I have no idea that I will experience the presence of God in the midst of my children, that holding each one and gazing amazed into their tiny soulful eyes is the thinnest of places. I wonder when tiny fingers entangle mine: Does she remember life inside me? Does he meet Jesus while he's being crafted in my womb?

But even more, I begin my lifelong struggle with worry. Will I be the mommy they need? And what if I'm not? I grasp for Jesus when I parent, not merely because I know my need, but because I have few examples of positive parenting growing up. I worry they will grow up without knowing they're cherished or loved or applauded. Those thoughts haunt me more than I am able to articulate. Will my children know I love them? I do not voice these fears—not even to my husband. These silent worries strangle me as I fall asleep, choking my joy.

The summer of 1999 changes all that. My friend Heidi spends a week with our family. Not knowing the monster of fear that grabs at my mommy thoughts, she says this to me. "Mary, your children know you love them."

God uses my observant friend to salve an unspoken wound. In that thin place, I taste God's grace. Heidi's words give freedom for the first time—freedom from guilt, tortured worry, and bound-up fear. Her words quiet the declarations in my head, those accusing words that scream, "You're not a good mother."

Enjoying my newfound emancipation, I begin to delve into the souls of my kids, try to understand them, be an observer. It's not long before I see something paradoxical. It's not that I'm raising my kids per se, it's that God is growing me up through my kids. He's whispering and reaching and tugging at my heart through my children. Dan Allender confirms this. "To the degree that we read our children as God wrote them, we will grasp the ineffable glory of what we are most meant to know and enjoy. God intends to reveal himself to us through our children as much as, if not more than, he intends for us to teach our children about him."[5]

And He reveals Himself through every child.

Through Sophie, I experience the evangelical heart of God. She longs to see people come to know Him, but in such an irresistible manner, it takes my breath away. Sophie comes home from youth group, her smile wider than the French skyline. "I have never felt closer to God," she says.

"How so?"

"Tonight I helped my friend meet Jesus!" She details the entire scene, updating me on her friends' questions and ultimate desire to take the biggest step of her life. The process takes over a year where Sophie prays constantly for her friend, answers theological questions with grace, and loves her friend who struggles with not fitting in at school.

I wrap my arms around my daughter. "Thank You, Jesus," I whisper. I thank Him because I see Him clearly in Sophie's shining eyes. And I experience Him.

Aidan's giving heart keeps me abreast of God's desire to bless His children. Aidan saves his money to give toward digging wells in Africa.

He calls his friend. "Um, I know this sounds strange, but can I talk to your parents?" He asks the parents if they'd bought their son an MP3 player for Christmas. His father says no. Aidan pesters Patrick about going to a particular store so he can buy his best friend an MP3 player. Watching Aidan wrap the extravagant gift bought with his own money sends shivers through me. Is this like God? Longing to surprise us with the desires of our hearts? Wanting to bless us beyond measure?

"The highlight of my day," Aidan tells us later, "was seeing my friend's face when he opened the gift." In that moment, I can almost see the veil between heaven and earth rip in two, revealing Jesus on the face of my son.

Julia's intrepid endurance of terrible school situations in France breaks my heart. Most days in the beginning she cries her way home. Her teachers are mean and cold, her friends nonexistent. Until she learns the language, my sweet verbal girl shuts down, having no outlet for her many, many words. It surprises me what she does say when French words touch her lips. She asks kids if they know God. She takes spiritual inventory of her entire class. And she shares Jesus with them using the little vocabulary she has. Such grit. Such pluck. Such endurance.

In that thin place of Julia's endurance, I understand Jesus. How He endures so much on this earth in order to save many. Now that she's blossoming in America, I feel the weight of those two and a half years, how they impact Julia today. She's tough. But she's even more loving. Oh, to be like that. To be lambasted only to bounce back and love some more.

I start my parenting journey with debilitating fear — cisterns full of it. I continue it now with holy anticipation of Jesus' presence, ever watching and waiting for a thin place to open up in the life of one of my children, lifting the gauzy veil between now and not yet. What I used to dread I now see as an adventure, not merely in child rearing, but in discovering God imprinted on the faces and souls of my children. After all, doesn't Jesus say we won't know Him rightly if we don't become like children? And how can stodgy old adults become kidlike unless we entangle our lives with children?

I'm a frail, needy mommy who doesn't parent perfectly. Which is why it humbles me when I realize God stoops to earth to save a wretch like me, just as He did with Sophie's friend. When God over-the-top blesses me as Aidan blesses his friend, showering me with His peace, joy, life, and hope. When He teaches me tenacity through Julia's own. Oh, the love pours out! It's almost too much.

And yet, it's enough.

23

Jim Elliot

Is there such a thing as an aspirational thin place?

In college, I read *Passion and Purity* by Elizabeth Elliot and make all sorts of vows to myself. About who I will date, how I will date, and who I want to be. And really, all I want to be then is Jim Elliot—the missionary martyr who spent his college years memorizing Greek verbs and Scripture, who dared to take risks for his faith.

I sing my availability to Jesus as I walk to my dorm from the library, imagining myself a missionary. I stand in lines at lunch with my homemade memory verses on a D-ring clip, flipping through them over and over again, rejoicing when I memorize another. I look down my nose at my partying Christian friends. I read my Bible backwards and forwards and align myself with friends who do the same. In short, I become what I think Jim Elliot is—only in the process, I become a living, breathing Pharisee.

Because I believe that Jesus will really only meet with me in the wee hours of the morning, I pull myself out of bed to pray and read my Bible. I spend at least an hour a day with Jesus. If I skip a day, that song from the Christian radio station haunts me with words like, "I missed my time with you, those moments together …" The entire day is ruined because of my slacker ways. I'm convinced that God stands in heaven, consternation on His chiseled face, holding a Quiet Time clipboard. "Well, she did it every day this month except today. Tsk. Tsk. Tsk." He pulls the page from my clipboard, then rips the page from top to bottom—just as the temple veil is torn—thus nullifying my entire month of quiet times because of my one lazy day.

I live a morality play, me being the chief character. But I'm so terribly naughty and weak and frail that I fail all the time.

Why am I this way? Why do I torture myself with rules aplenty?

For me, it boils down to upbringing. I grow up in the free-loving seventies where rules aren't in fashion. A generation of hippie parents believe that hedging kids in with top-down authority smacks of the machine they're raging against. So I grow up with very few rules. And, for someone like me who loves control, this freaks me out. So, what do I do? Make them up. Even this week, I catch myself constructing new rules to follow so I'll feel better, more in control. It's a lifelong problem for me.

Before I become a Christian, I write a daily list of things I must do in order to be good. Things like:

Brush teeth.
Comb hair.
Say one thing nice to a friend.
Do chores without complaining.
Smile more. (Aside: how can that be measured?)
Do homework.
Look for someone who is sad and cheer him or her up.
Write in diary.
Floss.

Be friendly.

Do not be mean to the neighbor girl, or make fun of her behind her back.

The list is actually quite extensive, centered on grooming and niceties, but I won't bore you with it. What's worse is ending my day with "my precious"—written in a Gollum scrawl—list. I look it over, congratulating myself for combed hair, bludgeoning myself for unflossed teeth and lack of smiles (maybe the two go hand in hand!). I cannot abide my mistakes. So I lecture myself in my head, telling the bad me to please remember the flossing regimen, and for heaven's sake smile once in a while at school. Or be kind to your neighbor who treats you like garbage at school only to love you when you're both home. Every night, I chastise myself. Every morning, I endeavor to be perfect.

But I never am.

That high-pitched taskmaster follows me into Christendom. I replace flossing with quiet times and continue the process of beating myself up every night for my failures. How can that possibly be beneficial to my soul? Why do I do such things?

One word: control.

I live in bits and pieces of chaos growing up. Since I cannot survive well in that chaos, I try my darnedest to order my world. I know I can't control circumstances or other people, so I figure I can at least control myself. Which brings me back to college and my Jim Elliot days.

Part of my legalism snaps blessedly in two when I go to Malibu (a Young Life camp in Canada) to attend a Young Life leadership retreat. Juan Carlos Ortiz, an Argentinean pastor, preaches from his book *Disciple*. For the first time in my life, I begin to glimpse freedom-loving Christianity. I am no longer married to the Law, he tells me, I'm married to Christ—and He's all about grace and freedom and truth. He opens my eyes and heart to verses like these:

"For the Law was given through Moses; grace and truth were realized through Jesus Christ" (John 1:17 NASB).

"It was for freedom that Christ set us free; therefore keep standing firm and do not be subject again to a yoke of slavery" (Galatians 5:1 NASB).

"Therefore, my brethren, you also were made to die to the Law through the body of Christ, so that you might be joined to another, to Him who was raised from the dead, in order that we might bear fruit for God" (Romans 7:4 NASB).

I feel the first birth pangs of liberation — that life is not about control or me following my own silly rules. It's about Jesus, and what He did on the cross. At Malibu, under British Columbia skies, I feel His presence and favor and joy like never before. If physical spots on this earth are measured to find thin places between God and man, I am convinced Malibu is one of the thinnest. In that mountain fjord, captured by words of freedom that seem too good to be true, I rest for one of the first times in my life.

But my newfound freedom is short-lived.

After college, I marry Patrick, then walk my slow descent toward gloom. I spend inordinate amounts of time comparing myself to my glory years in college where, in my opinion, I am Super Christian. As a schoolteacher, I don't do Quiet Times. I don't share Jesus at every turn. Although I sing to Him during my car ride to school and cry prayers to Him as I leave, I am convinced I'm a reprobate because I don't do what I used to do. I feel like a fallen Girl Pharisee — one who used to be piously rigorous only to find herself terribly lax. I forget all about Malibu, and refashion God into the perturbed deity in the sky, clipboard of my failures in hand.

I carry my legalistic self into homemaking, determining to be the perfect housewife who manages her home admirably. I berate myself not saving enough money as we live on one income, so I subscribe to the *Tightwad Gazette* and become obsessive. I read about garage sales, panicking if I don't get there when they open. I live in strange fear that some other garage saler will find something before I do, thus nullifying my quest. I time my husband while he shaves, secretly seething that he takes too long and wastes hot water. I wash tinfoil. I wear sweaters in winter to keep the thermostat low. I take quick showers. I shop at thrift bakeries. And at night, instead of basking in the warmth of the electric blanket my dear husband buys me, I shiver and fret about how I don't measure up.

Much more than my own inability to save the most money, I worry about my motherhood, how I don't spend enough time with my kids. I think of Jim Elliot, how he spends his life, and I worry that I'm too entrenched in suburbia to go overseas. In every way, I don't measure up. So many regrets assault me at night that I can't sleep and seldom feel at rest.

I meet a pastor friend who helps me discover what's wrong with me. Scott tells me, "Mary, you have an overactive conscience." When he describes my condition, I nod my head — as does my husband. Yep. All those to-do lists gone awry. All those sleepless nights recounting my failure. All those times I don't measure up to my ideal — whether that be Jim Elliot or Perfect Mary. All those times I apologize, though I don't need to. (I wonder how many times I make stuff up to be sorry about!) My conscience is on Millennium Falcon hyperdrive, and I can't seem to stop it.

But Jesus can.

He can and He does, but it's a slow, continual process.

A few years back in my journal I write, "I agonized over my

own tendency to sin to Jesus. He said, 'Pursue Me, not perfection. Follow after Me, not a set of ideals. Grab My hand and walk with Me in adventure.'" I grasp this now and again, but freedom eludes me like forgotten items on a discarded to-do list. This need to be free from Pharisee me is a lifelong pursuit, where I learn to crucify my own agenda of control in lieu of Jesus' presence in me. Oswald Chambers says this to taskmaster me: "We have put our sense of duty on the throne instead of the resurrection life of Jesus."[6]

Stupid, stupid hyperactive conscience! How it gets me in trouble. How it harangues me, stifles me, keeps me from experiencing Jesus. I'm so busy recounting my losses and failures, then determining to "do better" that I miss His capability inside me. I am so capable, so in control, that I miss His power. Oswald Chambers encourages an entirely different life: "Every element of self-reliance must be slain by the power of God. Complete weakness and dependence will always be the occasion for the Spirit of God to manifest His power."[7]

I get to the end of myself more often now. Before, I found this perturbing, but now understand it to be God's severe mercy. He loves me enough to show me how silly my lists are, how futile my self-flagellation is. He shows up in my need, my weakness — His paradoxical way of wooing me to His way of thinking. My way does not produce life in me. But when I acknowledge my need for Jesus, when I dare to let Him be my conscience, I experience that Malibu freedom all over again. His grace and peace dance on my empty stage. When I decorate the stage with my own props, things get convoluted. He cannot dance freely there.

God asks me to let go, to fling away, to trajectorize the me who criticizes myself to oblivion, the me who berates myself with I-should mantras. Though that me pummels myself, I'm hesitant to let her go. She's been my pharisaical security blanket.

Can I fling that me away—the me who keeps me in line, who makes sure I'm radical like Jim Elliot, who smashes any sense of pride and ensures the proper levels of humility? Who will God put in that place? Maybe wisdom? Maybe He'll bring me joy, peace, hope, and laughter. Or maybe just plain rest, which often eludes me.

The prospect terrifies me a bit.

I sense freedom in the distance. It echoes through the voice of Juan Carlos Ortiz in the evergreen Canadian wilderness, and beckons me further. I sense a great release on the horizon, but I'm not there yet.

24

The Blythe Constitution

I am nearly through with my college career, celebrating by attending a leadership conference at Malibu, the Young Life property in Canada. The scenery is breathtaking—inlets, fjords, mountains rising from glacial waters. I walk outside after a session, my head pounding. I am dizzy, sick to my stomach. I breathe in evergreen air, but it doesn't settle me.

New friends surround me. I steady myself on the railing overlooking the water below, but my knees jelly beneath me and I start falling. Someone catches me before I hit the ground.

I revel in the attention, so much so that I'm not entirely sure I would've fainted. How much of the weakness in my knees was my battle with bronchitis, and how much of it was my insatiable need for attention? It's a struggle that's taken a lifetime to sort through, my bent toward hypochondria.

One of the first two movies my husband and I rent together is *Anne of Green Gables* and *Anne of Avonlea*, the BBC Wonderworks production. Toward the end, when Gilbert is dying, Anne has a conversation in her room with Marilla. She tells her, "It's been a bad case from the start. No one's heard anything the past week. He has the Blythe constitution in his favor, though. If God wills it."[8]

That phrase worms its way through our married conversations, particularly when either of us is sick. But the truth is, I do not have the Blythe constitution. I have the Mary constitution, when, if compared to a literary character accurately, would be more like Ann de Bourgh, the sickly daughter of Lady Catherine de Bourgh in *Pride and Prejudice*.

As a child, dark hollows circle underneath my eyes. I am pale and often ill.

Something magical happens when I'm sick, though. I get attention. The world stops. My mom takes off work and spends the day nursing me. She pets my head, brings me broth, fusses over me. Though I wrestle with strep throat for years until my tonsils are blessedly yanked at fifteen, something in me cherishes sickness. I don't become a full-blown hypochondriac, but I sure come close — discovering sickness to be my ticket out of loneliness, my passport into the affections and empathies of family members.

Maybe this is why I always think I'm dying of cancer. My doctor, bless him, says I'm highly medically aware, which I'm sure makes him laugh when he's in his break room bantering with the nurses. I can launch a listing of ailments here, just like your Great Aunt Imelda does when you call her. But I'll spare you. I'll save that for when I'm old enough to merit such conversation. Like next week.

I call for Jesus five hundred times when I birth Julia without painkillers. I say His name over and over, asking Him why it hurts so much. My mom laughs. "Wow, it sounds like a big tent revival in here." Jesus. Jesus. Jesus. Of course, I worry I'll die. But Jesus is faithful. I live. Julia lives. And I keep calling His name when I'm in pain.

Once I legitimately think I'm dying. I have cramps, only to discover I can't stand up. I writhe on the floor of the emergency room — yes, on the germy floor — asking for Jesus to take me home, while my poor kids look at me with wide eyes. The diagnosis? Kidney stones. Though I don't die, I wish I do, particularly when the evil nurse gives me a crazy-big dose of painkiller that has me hallucinating lions and tigers attacking me.

My sickliness is a wonderful excuse not to exercise. Everything, really, becomes that excuse: too much studying, too busy with work, too many children to take care of, too many desires not to exercise. Battling the wimp demon is a lifelong struggle, one I capitulate to often.

Only recently I've become adamant about exercise. I train for a triathlon. Haunted by my own lack of athletic prowess, I take baby steps-strokes-pedals, convinced I'll never make it. But, I do make it, red faced and tired. And I intend to make it again.

I feel healthy, particularly when I'm running. It's my near-daily thin place where I hear Jesus' voice, experience His creation, and work out my woes under a sun-pierced sky.

Though I don't have the Blythe constitution growing up, I have it now, thanks to God's gracious provision and a shift in attitude. I no longer have to be sick to be loved. I no longer equate infirmary with someone's tender care. I see sickness as plain old malady, not a ticket to affection. I don't like sickness much. I want to wave a magic wand when my kids are sick, eradicating sickness forever.

Infirmities, though, are part of this crazy fallen world. I can't buy the health-and-wealth message that God wants us all to be chipper and sickness-free all our days because I learn a lot when

I'm sick. Like how to trust God in the midst of it. Or how to be joyful in any circumstance. Or how to exercise kindness when I don't feel like being nice to anyone. Or how to long for heaven where there will be no sickness. All good lessons.

Being sick does two things to me: it plunges me into the arms of Jesus, and it worries me that I'll be carried into the arms of Jesus through the gates of heaven. It's the strangest of thin places — a push-me, pull-me irony. And in a funny twist, exercising, particularly running, is a consistent thin place where I understand the importance of working out my no-longer-a-wimp status. It's my faith with running shoes on. I continue to be hyper-aware of my own health, though I am happily free of hypochondria. But when I grow crotchety and little hairs sprout on my chin, I pray I will run to Jesus, that I will exude Him when I'm frail, and that I will laugh my way through pain.

I think that's just how Gilbert Blythe would want it.

25

Running

He chases me in my night terrors. A dark man with red eyes, like Stephen King's villain in *The Stand*. I scream from five-year-old lungs, rattling the house. I tell my mom and my grandparents about the very real man chasing me through alleyways. Thirty-five years later, I still see one of the dreams like it's a movie. I am panting, faint from running. I bend over at the waist, my hands on my knees. A hand touches my shoulder. I scream, but nothing comes out. I run through the dark, not seeing where I'm going. He hisses that he will kill me. I run on, though my diaphragm heaves in a side ache. We near the water's edge. A long pier materializes before me. I run on the wooden planks, my blonde hair streaming behind me as his heavy bootsteps shake the boards. I stand at the end of the pier, facing him. He stops. He raises a gun to my chest and shoots. I recoil, feeling my rib cage disintegrate. Then I fall backwards, toward inky water. I bolt upright in bed, wild-eyed and screaming.

I spend a good deal of time running through my childhood, embodying the fear in my dream. One day I walk with a friend toward a grocery store that is about a mile from home. I am five. The sky starts to darken while the grocery store seems farther still.

We turn back, half running, half walking toward home. Though no one chases me, I feel enemies lurking behind every bush.

I am the girl who looks behind. Who makes up things to be afraid of. In third grade, I walk to and from school. I am convinced every car whizzing past holds a kidnapper, ready to slow down and offer me candy. I fancy the world one big circus of stranger danger. When I make it home, safe and sound, I worry about our broken lock, how I can easily jimmy it. If I can, so can killers, right?

My grandmother seems to know this about me. She hears my fears, though I don't tell them. Every day after school, after unlocking the nearly broken lock, my first task is to call her, to assure her I made it home safe and sound. Her voice calms my worries, but it can only reach so far through a telephone line.

When darkness falls, and I'm alone as a grade-schooler, I freak out. Every little creak of our old house startles me. I turn off the lights and peer into our treed yard following shadows with my eyes while my stomach screams fear. I suck in far too many breaths worrying that someone out there will pound on the door, break it down, and nab me.

It's strange how that killing-man in my dreams chases me throughout my life. It's uncanny how far I run, only to turn around and see his sickly grin, his red eyes. He follows me throughout my elementary school years, particularly when boys and men see my mark and try to take advantage of me—again. He lurks outside my bedroom window when I'm alone in high school. He feeds my fright in college when my roommate is nearly raped just four hundred feet from our dorm room, and when another friend is stalked. He is near when I'm on my own for the first time and can't stand being in the apartment alone. He feeds me morsels of anxiety when I'm newly married and my husband is out of town.

Eventually, I slow my run, but I am still vigilant, even now that I have three kids and can sleep in the house when my husband's gone. But sometimes I wake up afraid, having suffered again in a nightmare.

Since I've spent so much of my life running from specters unseen, and enemies seen, I have a hard time embracing the encouragers in my life. I so weary myself by running and fretting that I seldom slow down long enough to enjoy the people with which God has populated my life. Running from enemies will do that—blur my vision to the heroes God has given me.

I could spend a lifetime recounting villains; and in the recollection, I'll suffer runner's cramp. So much running. So much fear. But the thin place I've found where I experience the presence of Jesus like a whisper of a kiss from a breeze is this: wherever my husband is. He is my thin place because he's the hero I run to. I've come to see that running toward someone, particularly a hero, is much less exhausting than running from someone you can't see. Patrick is tangible. His love toward me is restorative. He points me to the True Hero, Jesus, whose love is without condition.

I know it the moment I see him for the first time. He is kneeling before an injured pastor, praying for his healing. Through a series of mishaps, we finally meet face-to-face, only to be separated for three months while Patrick works at Mother Teresa's Home for the Dying and Destitute in Calcutta, India. He experiences Jesus there, writes me letters about his encounters. I fall in love with Patrick's heart for Jesus and the poor. We start dating December 30 during the year of our Lord 1989 and marry one day shy of a year later on December 29, 1990.

Patrick makes me laugh, which makes running from my enemies difficult—I'm too distracted by the hilarity.

He holds me when our first pregnancy ends prematurely.

He rejoices when our children screech their way into the world. He holds them. Coos over them. Changes diapers.

He hears the Holy Spirit tell him, "You need to be there for your wife," when I have to do a relationally difficult thing. Though I face an enemy of sorts, he shelters me, listens to me, and protects me from the onslaught.

He is broken in all the right places so Jesus can shine through him, but he's strong where I'm weak.

He is theologically astute. His mind fascinates me.

He shepherds people; he can't help it. And he shepherds our family with grace and wisdom.

He gives me great gifts.

He takes me away on adventures, always the perfect vacation planner.

He is a man of honor who gladly wears the mantle of provider.

He makes me feel safe.

It takes me much of our seventeen-year marriage to completely stop running. To stop looking behind me with fretting eyes. And when I stop, I see Patrick, entreating me to slow down, holding my face, beckoning me to rest in the arms of Jesus.

I'm so very tired of running.

I'd rather rest in my husband's arms than spend my life fleeing unseen pursuers. In one of the most life-altering conversations I have with my husband, he says these words: "Mary, I know you've had a difficult life. It's my goal to make sure that the rest of your life is far better than the first bit." He washes my fear with those words. He takes my place, protecting me. I no longer have to look behind me with a hero like this. I can rest.

Patrick makes mistakes, as I do too. He's not a perfect hero; but he points me to Jesus, who is. Because my husband loves me and seeks my welfare, I'm better able to understand Jesus' love for me in ways I never understood before I was married. Much of what God does in my life is healing the past in order to embrace the future. He heals my fear of enemies so I will embrace my family. He heals my fear of men so I can embrace my husband. He heals my running so I can stop and notice the beauty of today.

The thin place between running from enemies and running toward a Hero is the love of Jesus made evident through my husband.

Mind if I rest in his arms a while?

26

Investigations

I'm not good living in mystery, so I fancy myself an investigative reporter, searching for clues and nuances of my past. Maybe I'm trying to be a little god, managing my universe, figuring out every detail. Or maybe I'm just plain curious. Or maybe that's why I write fiction, to iron out the mysteries, to control the story world.

I don't wrestle with the memories of my sexual abuse like you might think. Through the years God graciously stitches up the gaping wounds carved into my heart. But sometimes I wonder. What happened to those boys? They grew up to be men, right? What sort of men? Jailed? Successful but tormented? As normal as your next-door neighbor?

I'm into my late thirties when someone drops a clue, letting out the boys' last name—all quite by accident. I wander the Internet as a reporter might. The name is like the maddening game you get in a gum ball machine where little steel balls form a word or a picture by plopping into cardboard holes. I roll their last name around, hoping it will roll into a solid memory of that name.

Nothing.

I search for the name. It's an unusual one. I look for men near my hometown and find several. A guy who works outside for a living. A sculptor. A renowned doctor. A gay porn writer whose Amazon rankings are better than mine. (Oh the injustice!) An attorney. A dentist. An environmentalist.

I click on one of the names, which links me to an email address. How do I begin? "Um, yeah, when you were a young teen did you live in such and such a place? Did you know Eva the chain-smoking babysitter? Oh, and by the way ... " No, I can't type it. Even Reporter Mary can't type it.

I contact the local paper hoping to find a lead, only to pull away. I ask questions about the statute of limitations. It's not that I want them punished. After all, I forgive them, over and over, like a pardon mantra in my head. It's that I want to know what boys like that turn into. Do they find Jesus? Are they remorseful? Haunted? Have they blocked it from their memories? Or do they play their abuse over and over in their heads like a sick rerun?

In a fortuitous twist of timing, my daughter interrupts my clue-finding, asking about an Edgar Allen Poe story. "The Cask of Amontillado" is about revenge, of a man bricking up a wall while his enemy screams behind it. I don't want to be that character. I don't want to become a bitter bricklayer. But the curious part of me needs to find out what happens behind the wall.

In my mind I see reconciliation. I'm shaking hands with these brothers. They're weeping and begging forgiveness. I grant it, but walk away. It's enough for me to know they're full of baggage, that they're sorry.

Life is a lot like investigative reporting. We chase dead ends. We try to piece together the picture of our past like master puzzle doers. But some pieces are forever missing, and the remaining picture stares back at us, jagged, unfinished.

It heartens me to read these words in the *Dallas Morning News*. A. M. Homes, author of *The Mistress's Daughter*, writes her memoir as a way to reconstruct the puzzle of her life: The reporter writes: "As a novelist, Ms. Homes understands the power of adding or subtracting a detail in a story. She understands that such subtle changes alter a character. And as an adoptive daughter, she has learned that each time she is given another fragment of her life narrative, her identity is subtly shifted, too."[9] Some would say I need to let the past be incomplete. I agree. But the reporter in me has to piece the fragments together before I move on. At least that's what I think I need.

Heaven helps me when I'm in these perplexing places. As a storyteller, I love happy endings, plot points tied up neatly, relationships resolved. I'd like to think that heaven's beauty comes from God finishing our stories there. This world is unraveled; but perhaps in the next world, we'll finally see a rhyme and a reason for our seemingly chaotic lives. It's my hope that He will complete my puzzled picture with pieces that suddenly make sense in light of eternity.

In that tension of the now and the not yet, I find a thin place. God comes near and whispers,

> *Will you trust Me with your fragments?*
> *With the missing pieces?*
> *Do you believe I am big enough to hold the mystery?*
> *Can you let Me be the Investigative Reporter,*
> *The Editor in Chief?*
> *All this needing-to-know*
> *Is holding you back*
> *From living in the now of today*
> *It tethers you to the past.*
> *Let it go,*
> *Not on a fickle breeze,*

But into My capable hands
Because I hold mysteries
And I hold yours.

In the past I needed all the fragments of my life placed just so, like diamonds set in a tennis bracelet. The older I get, the more I see that Jesus wants me to trust Him for the missing pieces, the broken clasps, the counterfeit baubles — to relax in the unknowing, to be at peace with the tangles, to learn the art of living with the mystery. He is more than capable of handling all my questions, and someday He will make things right. "I'm thanking God, who makes things right. I'm singing the fame of heaven-high God" (Psalm 7:17 MSG).

27

Liquor

Alcohol freaks me out.

I grow up in an extended family that drinks a lot. As a child, I often don't hear them say they love me unless they're drunk. It comes out slobbery—the kind of fake affection that churns my stomach. Sometimes I'm afraid when I'm riding in the car with someone who's had too much to drink. As the car swerves left and right, I worry I'll die. When parties get out of control, I run to my room, holding my knees to my chest, rocking.

I stay away from alcohol for good reason—until eighth grade when my friend invites me to her party, which is really quite small. The boy I like will be there, she says. "And we'll be drinking," she entices.

I worry all week. Will I like it? Will I say no? Will I look like a fool if I protest?

In the dark of her guesthouse, she hands me a Rainier beer. It's cold. It tastes like carbonated pee. The carbonation makes me burp, but I keep drinking, hoping it will get better. I drink three of them and feel dizzy, woozy, and out of control. I do ridiculous things.

I decide drinking is not my thing. I hate feeling out of control, and I particularly don't like the headache I have the next day.

I drink a few more times in early high school. Every time I feel absolutely stupid and regret my actions immediately.

So when I meet Jesus, I am blessedly free to say no to the demon liquor. Jesus doesn't want me drunk, right? So it's as easy as pie to say no. Later in high school, my friend Abigail and I feel exactly the same way about alcohol. We make fun of folks who drink. We secretly scold our Christian friends who do.

At one party, we hide away in a room because all our Christian friends are wasted on alcohol and we feel uncomfortable. We share a kinship there, eventually leaving together, laughing at our friends and their sloshed ways.

But in college, Abigail discovers alcohol. She falls in with a new crowd who take her down an entirely different path. I see Abigail's hollow eyes. She averts her gaze from me, perhaps because of shame. And for too long of a time, I stay in that place of anger. How dare she break our vow of alcohol abstinence?

Thankfully, I separate my hatred of alcohol from my friendship with Abigail, and we walk the tenuous path of reconciliation. The last time I see her, her eyes are clearer, as if she's seen the path of newfound addiction and it's sobered her up. We talk casually, almost the friendly laughter-filled banter we remember from high school. I hug her tight and we talk of our next reunion.

I am home from college for a short break when my mom gets a phone call.

"Abigail's dead," she tells me. "Flipped her car."

I shake my head no. I can feel her embrace, that beckoning of renewed friendship we shared just a fraction of time before. Dead? My dear friend?

She was driving her car too fast, under the influence. A tire hit the side of the road where gravel knocked it off kilter. The car flipped, and she was projected outward.

The church is packed. A sea of friends and family cram into the large auditorium. She's had an influence on many, I see. I suck in a breath before standing at the pulpit. Tears still wet my face, but I pray for a clear voice to say the words I wish I didn't have to say.

She reclines in her coffin, her eyes closed over by a mortician, her skin as cold as a tile floor. I look at her a long moment before starting to speak. She is dead, right in front of me. I nearly choke. Stupid, stupid booze.

I talk about her. How funny she is—was. How full of life. How smart. How she is—was—a good friend. I talk about Jesus, the Resurrected One, and for a brief moment, while she sleeps in front of me, her face the color of copy paper, I wonder if Jesus will pull a Lazarus. Will He lift the lid covering her broken body and tell her to come forth? Every inch of me wills it so. But she doesn't open her eyes.

I sing a song over my dead friend. The melody lifts over the weeping congregation—a song about sorrow, how we can't always know why, how God's ways are wider than the sky. I crack on the very last note, descend the platform, and weep into a heap, while Abigail's mouth says nothing.

When she is lowered into the ground, my hatred for alcohol seethes.

The night I wake up to laughter and mayhem at the end of my dorm hallway, I almost welcome my rage. Hair askew, I approach the open door of one of my wing mates. They're having a rip-roaring party, with booze aplenty—something forbidden on campus, something I, as the Resident Assistant, have to enforce. How dare they break the rules? I feel personally insulted, as if I personify the rules and they've decided to drink to both. In a rare fit of rage, I grab a beer bottle, holler a slew of words, then fling it to the other end of the room. The girls look at me, wide-eyed. The room is silent, except for a stifled sound: giggles.

That's how mad I get at alcohol. It's as if I see a group of people downing it for pleasure and I am suddenly thrust back, unwillingly, to parties of the past where I feel afraid and small, not knowing what the unpredictable adults will do. I evade the demon liquor through college and marriage. I have a conversation with another married couple early in our marriage. "I will never, ever touch the stuff," I brag.

But then God calls us to France. I finally relax my stance on alcohol, realizing Jesus turned water to wine, not into grape juice as some of my churchy friends believe. If He did that, wine can't be entirely evil. I have an occasional glass of wine with dinner, trying to prepare myself for a nation who will think it nutty if I don't drink wine. I still don't really like it, but I do my best.

Partway through our stint in France, a family visits us. They are missionaries in Eastern Europe and the wife is the older sister of my deceased friend Abigail. We spend good time recounting Abigail's life, grieving, and delving beyond her death to our lives today. It's a life-affirming time, a unique bookend to a painful journey.

Two years later, the phone rings. I'm never ready for death calls, and this day is no different. A family member is found dead in his apartment, alcohol partly to blame. He's been dead thirty-six hours when his parents discover him there.

He will never sing again on this earth. Alcohol stole that from him. Or maybe better put: he let himself be robbed by it. He battled alcohol and drugs his entire adult life, and it won.

At his funeral, I am grieved and angry. I want to kick the demon liquor in its decaying teeth. But really all I can do is pray. And cry. Guns shoot blanks into the crisp sky, honoring his life.

A flag is folded, handed to his parents. A prayer is prayed, a sermon given. Standing there, I remember a picture, faded black and white with deckled edges. It's a baby sitting on someone's knee. A beer bottle is lifted to baby lips, the caption reading "Little Drunkard."

That image is a mournful thin place for me—a prediction of what could be, of what ends up becoming. I shudder to think what would happen if I ever gave myself over to the demon liquor. Knowing my all-or-nothing personality, and seeing that folks often drink to cover up pain, I no doubt would've nursed the stuff until it killed me, from little drunkard to big drunkard to dead drunkard in a matter of years. It's a thin place, this photo, because it reminds me of God's rescue, how He whispers one million I-love-yous over me, woos me to Himself so I won't turn to something artificial to fill me up. It's a thin place because now I am intoxicated by Jesus, forever changed, forever filled.

I do not throw beer bottles anymore. I do not judge others who choose to drink more frequently than I am comfortable with. I even drink an occasional glass of wine. But I still don't embrace alcohol—not for theological reasons, but for social ones. When relatives slur their love for me only under the influence, when adults do stupid out-of-control things after too many beers, when people I love endanger themselves and others because of an addiction, I don't understand.

Maybe my lack of understanding is an indication that I need more healing. Or maybe it's plain old wisdom. Or maybe it's part of this crazy life we live, part of the fabric of society that we need to weave in and out of.

Sometimes I'm still that little girl who smells alcohol on her relative's breath, who feels the crushing weight of a hug given under the influence.

Sometimes I'm singing bewildered over Abigail's coffin.

Sometimes I'm having a drink with friends, wondering what the big deal is.

Sometimes I weep over the demon liquor's stronghold over folks.

But always I'm reminded that we who navigate earth are needy people who sometimes turn to other things to cope.

28

Marked

At first I don't realize those boys who violate me at five leave themselves behind. They etch on me an indelible mark — the kind sexual predators see, like a fluorescent tattoo under black light. Though I am safe from those two, I am never *entirely* safe.

During parties my parents have, I stay tucked away in my bedroom, hoping no one will come in, but frantic fear grips me as the clock ticks on into the night and the party grows fangs and people get stupid.

Later I'm lured to the back of an old tree house, on my step-grandparents' property by the promise of play. A boy spies my mark. "We're going to do surgery. You know, play doctor," he says.

Though I'm world savvy by this time in my elementary career, I don't yet know the lingo — that playing doctor is akin to being brutalized again. I honestly think I'll get to be a nurse or a patient or a doctor.

Boy One starts to pull down his pants. Boy Two holds me from behind.

When I see Boy One do such a thing, I nearly throw up. I look around for anyone to save me, but there is no one. Certainly not Boy Two whose fingers press bruises into my upper arms. I know that if someone is going to save me, it has to be me. But to be honest, I'm weary of being my own parent, yet not so weary that I want these boys to do what they intend to do. Laughter rings through the backyard where cousins play happy games, but my voice gets stuck in my throat, just like in my dreams where killers chase me and I scream air. I am dead silent. And for a moment, I cannot do anything but shake beneath the grip of Boy Two behind me.

Boy One moves closer. I do the best thing I know to do. I fight. Kick. Wrestle. Struggle. Kick some more. I break free and scramble down the ladder. I take advantage of my opportunity and run away, while the waistband of Boy One's pants form a temporary shackle around his legs and Boy Two rubs his shins.

I never, ever go into that tree house again. But I don't tell a soul what happened. It would be a ball of tangled yarn — if I pull out this episode, the other one will have to come undone and I will have to face something more terrifying still: what if my family doesn't care? I keep things quiet because I can't bear the thought of sharing my story and facing indifference. Better to keep alive the illusion that my family will all be shocked and angry, though my boiling fear keeps me believing no one will give a rip if they know. And I'll still have to fend off boys, still have to try in vain to erase my mark.

No, it's best to keep these secrets hidden away. For safekeeping.

In the silence of my secret, the mark seems to grow and glow, attracting more predators.

My father exposes me to others' nudity in a lifestyle that is less than safe. A boy finds me cleaning stalls in our barn. He moves closer. I run. I babysit at a farm where an irresponsible brother can't take care of his younger sister. He follows me, sweet talks me, though I'm barely an adolescent. He moves closer. I shake. "I like you," he tells me. He wraps strong arms around me. My stomach groans in fear. By some sort of miracle, I wriggle my way free.

I'm convinced I'm marked. I emit some sort of signal that invites sexual deviants to try their hand at me. When I meet Jesus, I expect the mark to leave. It doesn't.

A boyfriend puts his hand on my shoulders as he stands behind me. My palms turn to sweat. He moves his hands toward my chest. I jump up, quick as a fox, and break up with him.

I am eighteen when a man leers at me, tells me how good I look in my swimsuit, follows me around, tries to touch me. I can see in his forty-year-old eyes that he has no good intentions. I hide.

A married, much-older pastor makes advances toward me. I am brave enough to confront him. He backs away.

I battle what the mark has done to my soul. I believe that my worth has more to do with how I look to men than who I am in Jesus. In a strange reversal, I no longer run from those bent on violating me as much as I long for an admiring look. I actually believe that spilling my sordid story will attract men, that is, until I tell a guy in my dorm — a real catch. For a while he seems interested, until I spew out all the details. His eyes widen as if he's seen the mark for the first time. He advises counseling, even gives me a counselor's phone number.

This battle torments me in high school and college. I'm involved in the strangest courting dance in history:

I catch his attention, which feels great.

He pursues.

I am still happy, but my stomach starts churning.

He makes a declaration.

I run one hundred miles the other way.

I call it the push-me-pull-me dating method of Mary. I perplex myself and my potential dates in this dance.

And then I get married. The mark goes away, allowing me to live happily ever after.

But it doesn't.

And I don't.

This excruciating sexual abuse mark follows me right into the marriage bed. By God's surprising grace, I enter that bed a virgin, but completely freaked out. That shameful and violating act is now suddenly permissible? Couple that with the taboos associated with sex and my own hard-won freedom from pornography and you have a screwed up girl, desperately wanting to be whole. Or normal.

I long to rejoice in the marriage bed. And I do. I'm not so wounded that I can't enjoy God's gift of sex — this is truly a miracle. But way down deep, where the mark of sexual abuse has had its way with my soul, I am broken. I battle wondering if that's all I'm good for, if sex is what defines my worth. I feel used easily. And though I have a patient, loving husband, it is never easy for me to let go. He and I both feel burglarized by those boys, stripped down and bare. They have stolen much more than my innocence; they've taken my sense of wholeness, warped my view of sex.

The mark makes me think strange things — like if I enjoy sex now, I legitimatize my abusers back then. I share this with my husband and he tries to understand. All I can do is pray Jesus heals this wound, because it's not yet fully healed.

I attend a conference about being sexually available to my husband. I hear women give testimony to their newfound sex life and how we should choose days of the week to have sex so our husbands will be happy with us. I'm told to think about sex all day long in preparation for "the night."

I look around the auditorium. It's packed with woman leaning forward in their pews, scratching notes, nodding heads. I wonder if I'm the only one there who feels violated and terrified. I pray for the other people like me in the congregation, women so tortured by memories of the past that they can't think of sex as beautiful. It takes everything inside them to elevate it to the status of duty. I ache for these women.

Then I get mad. The folks running the conference have no ill intentions, but they are blind to the 25–30 percent of women who have been violated. They are heaping an unrealistic burden on already broken backs.

Leaving that conference, my eyes are downcast, lids heavy with yet another weapon to punish myself with. I'm not the wife my husband needs me to be. I'm not enough. I must work harder. I must try to overcome the sick feeling in my gut because now I'm not only required to do the act but to truly engage my soul in it. How in the world do I do that?

I realize I cope by disengaging. Although I am blessed to be one of the few who can stay married, can enjoy sex, and is not in a string of broken relationships or plagued by the opposite — too many random sexual encounters that deaden the soul — I am not really there. To cope with my very real feelings of disgust and violation, I disconnect from the act. My body enjoys sex, but my mind is somewhere else, disengaged. At times I feel that my husband's expectations for me to engage wholeheartedly — heart, soul, mind, emotions — are unfair and impossible. I pray often to be an engaged wife, but my prayers seem to go unanswered. This is something I cannot do; I know that. But it's also something Jesus hasn't seen fit to heal me from.

That terrible mark is still burned into my soul.

Never is that starker to me than when I purchase a product from a ministry that is supposed to help us be romantic. The premise: take turns planning a date night. The man's arsenal includes all sorts of romantic adventures—dates, flowers, surprises. But the wife's cards deal almost exclusively with sex. A few I consistently place at the back of the pile; they are simply too hard for me to do. I cannot put fruit on my belly to be eaten off by my husband. The thought of being laid bare like that makes me want to vomit. Though I have experienced a massive amount of healing in this area, I still cannot bring myself to entice. I can't play games or expose myself that way. It's not a dogged refusal on my part, maliciously plotting to deny my husband what he needs or deserves. It's pure inability. I cannot do these things. And I resent other Christians telling me that I must or I'm not the godly woman I'm supposed to be. I'd much rather have grace than sexy wife rules. I'd much rather hear date suggestions from folks who've been violated and know that asking those things can be soul damaging and traumatic. I'd rather find a book that helps husbands or wives of spouses who have been violated better love their marked partners. Why, why, why does it boil down to me having to do the impossible? What about grace?

How can the mark of sexual abuse be a thin place? Could such a place exist, where God intervenes and interjects His beauty into something so terribly grotesque? I hope so. I have caught glimpses of Him there, though I rail against Him for not removing the mark forever. I've spewed one million *whys* to the heavens, cried one billion tears in agony. I've shouted "It's not fair!" more times than I can count. In those moments I rest in one thing: God's sovereignty. It's not pretty. It's not easy to believe, especially when I dive into raw questions like, "What kind of loving Father would allow His baby girl to go through so much abuse?" It's not intuitive. It doesn't smack of justice. But it's there.

God holds the cosmos in His hands. And, though there are days I wonder if I'm a disembodied spirit belonging to no one,

I am in His hands—the hands that are marked in blood with my own mountain of sins. The hands, feet, and heart that bore the sins of those two boys who walk this earth as haunted men. The naked, violated One who hung on a cross so I could be set free from this ugliness. I'm captured at the sight of Jesus up there on the cross. I see my own agony etched across His face. I watch Him shoulder my mark and the marks of far too many boys and girls around this world who succumb to gazing heavenward for redemption and release.

Some days, that's enough. Even so, it's a struggle.

I give away the box of dates that was supposed to be so much fun for my husband and me, and cower in my unworthiness. I'm no Proverbs 31 woman, no godly helpmeet—all because of that insipid mark and my inability to erase it.

Amazing Life

Folks may wonder why I've spent all this time looking back, dredging up what God sees of my story, what my eyes see. Jesus says truth sets people free. This is my way of doing that—of telling the stark truth on the page so others can be set free. How can painful memories be a thin place?

Why do I go through all this recollection?

So God can renew me so I can help others find healing.

In 2 Corinthians 1, Paul says this: "Blessed be the God and Father of our Lord Jesus Christ, the Father of mercies and God of all comfort, who comforts us in all our affliction so that we will be able to comfort those who are in any affliction with the comfort with which we ourselves are comforted by God" (vv. 3–4 NASB).

Never do these verses become so alive to me than when I receive an email from a mother of an adopted girl, six, who hears about my story on the radio. She'd been molested before coming to her new family. The mom writes, "Helen heard part of [your story], enough to understand that your pasts were probably somewhat similar. She sat on my lap and laid her head on my shoulder and said that it was 'sad that no one saved you like she was saved' and that she was 'sorry you had to live your whole life like that.' We prayed for you, and I tried to explain to her that you were saved by Jesus. She didn't seem to get it. A little while later, I heard Barbara [her eldest adopted daughter with a similar past] talking to Helen about how she thought God had protected you because you were supposed to help girls like them. She said that it sucks that kids go through bad times, but if no one big had ever gone through it before and been okay, then there would be no one to help them."

The memories still sting, though less now. Life is bittersweet. I can thank God for being the patient, steady parent I needed, and especially for taking my tragedy and — turning it into triumph — not for me to trumpet my own resilience to the world, but for Him to take the likes of me, a five-year-old afraid to say a swear word, and use me to help the Helens and Barbaras of the world.

As I write, I am Hagar, Sarai's handmaiden, lost in the wilderness of my life, feeling alone and helpless. And, as it did for Hagar, my comfort comes in the form of two words: God sees.

Hagar names God; she is the only one to do so. In that place of destitution — alone and afraid — she calls Him El Roi, the God who sees. These two words carry me through this bewildering life. Hagar's name means flight. How many times have I flown from life's mess, only to weep in the desert? How many times have I wondered whether God sees? To be honest, it's often hard for me to believe that His eyes trace over the story of my life.

He sees me toddling in poverty, watches me hiding in my room when wild parties frighten me at five.

He sees our home ransacked by burglars at seven, how I tremble in bed.

He watches me walk to school third through fifth grade, sees me when I run from perceived bullies.

He hovers over my father's funeral while folks clad in black hug me tight.

He watches as Derek plants a slobbery first kiss on my reluctant lips in the Chalet Theater.

He notices how my stomach curls in on itself, how utterly terrified I am of men, and yet how desperately I need their approval and affection.

He watches me through junior high when life seems unlivable.

He sees me cry streams, rivers, oceans.

He smiles down on me as I weep my invitation to Him to be my everything at fifteen.

He watches me bumble my way through high school, pining for a boyfriend.

He sees my friends pray for me in college. He sends bucketfuls of healing my way.

He notices when I spy my not-yet husband in a crowd at church and watches over our courtship.

He sees me walking down the wedding aisle on my grandfather's arm.

He sees my struggles as a young mother, how very inadequate I feel.

He watches as Patrick and I navigate marriage's minefields.

He notices it all, every move, every heartache, every small victory, every leap of faith, every adventure, every bit of drudgery in the mundane. He sees. A recent poem captures how awestruck I am at the God who sees.

> *It's You whose eyes do see the earth*
> *Gently gliding over mirth*
> *Breathing life and giving birth*
> *Enlivening hearts, embracing dearth*

I trudge, then fall, then stagger to You
Whose eyes do roam above the view
Who sees the forest and the dew,
Watches decay, yet makes anew

Sustaining me, the God Who Sees
My sapling life beneath the trees
From underbrush and thorns, He frees
The brokenness of all my pleas

O stalwart God, perplexing One
Whose incandescence is my sun
That lights the path I have to run
Though on the road, I come undone

Unwound like balls of fickle string
I crash inside, but long for spring
Until the day I choose to sing
And ride upon Your carrier wing

You carry me, a broken bird
Under pinions, without word
My soul You green, my hope You gird
And all my pain becomes absurd

You see it all; You see it all
When I rise and when I fall
Sheltering under trees too tall
And You will see me when I call
And I will see You when You call.

In reading through old college journals, I'm amazed Jesus not only sees me, but He skillfully intersects my life. I ache as I read. I have similar struggles today as I did in university land — they're just couched a little differently. As I read, I worry about what I write and consider the incinerator. I'm raw on the page, even then — laid bare before myself and the God who sees it all. I am ruthless with myself when my pen scribbles on paper. Mother Teresa's desire to destroy her private writings resonates with me. What if everyone knows every single piece of darkness in my soul?

Jesus surprises me, being naked on that cross. I've been naked, and I've wrestled with the nudity I've exposed on the page. I've deleted words. I've added a few. Sometimes I wonder if I'm trying too hard to look, as Anne Lamott puts it, Jesusy. I'm just like you. So needy. So broken. So bewildered and shaken. My mind is occupied far too much with petty things. I look for acceptance everywhere, fueled by a hyper need for validation and positive strokes. I neglect. I gossip. I covet. I am self-absorbed.

But as I read these journals I see something startling: my heart. Bleeding all over those journals twenty years younger, a pattern emerges. I am insanely in love with Jesus Christ. I trip up and harbor a terribly fickle heart, but even in my straying, He's constantly on my mind. Pen to paper, I shower Him with affectionate words. I scribble His messages to me. I devour the Bible and memorize its beauty. God sees me, and I also see Him. And love Him.

If I throw all the journals out, my reputation will be safer, won't it? No one will know the depth of my depravity. No one will have the fodder to expose my soul to the world like a spiritual muckraker. All true. But they also won't see a wrestling pilgrim, following painstakingly after Jesus. No one will see the portrait of the girl who falls down, then gets up. The grace that shines brighter on a darkened life will seem duller without my darkness. And maybe I'll be tempted — if I throw away my journals — to stand a little taller, believing that somehow I corrected myself, that I became free by my own doing.

No. The journals will stay, though I say so with fear and trembling. Because the ultimate Author of my life is Jesus. He has taken a frail, needy, empty girl and helped her to dance. And even when she stumbles badly and makes a mess of her life, He still sees her, loves her, woos her, delights in her. It's one of the grandest mysteries of my life — that God can watch my life, read those journals, and still love me. And the second grandest mystery will be in chapter two of my life: when I finally believe that He does. Once and for all.

Funny how I can believe that for everyone else in my life, but can't extend that grace to myself. Jesus loves me. Jesus loves me. Jesus loves me.

And I absorb His presence in every thin place:

> *Why are the streets*
> *Dry after all that rain?*
> *How can they be?*
> *It's like my soul*
> *In times like these*
> *Washed one moment*
> *Parched the next*
> *I guess I need You*
> *Raining on me constantly*
> *Or I'll dry clear up*

On my run I spy a bird way up high, perched on the top branch of a tall Texas tree. He sings there, whistling to the sky. The bird is a metaphor from God to me. The bird can soar. He's grown accustomed to the vista, to seeing the world from way up there. So when he rests, he takes the highest place.

I want to fly to the treetop, my body bending the highest branch. I know that when I'm rooted to the earth my troubles seem mountainous. When I fly toward the heavens I remember the times I soar in worship or experience what my friend Helen calls the kiss of the King. My problems seem smaller up there on that branch. Maybe it's the God's-eye view of things, a more balanced perspective from above the earth. Or maybe it's because I'm living in that great expectation of God when I'm way up high. Or maybe because I experience God in that thin place between earth and sky.

It's enough to make me pray:

Jesus, the tree's so tall and I'm so small. I don't have wings. But You can fly wingless me to the treetop. Help me reach the higher branches so I can sing. Help me know You see me. Enliven me. Reach me. Help me gain Your perspective, experience Your presence. I want to fly, want to have an amazing life. But even more than that, I want to know You every single day. Give me wings, yes. But give me eyes to see the thin places life brings me, whether I'm soaring or glowering or laughing.

That's what I want to be — a Jesus-follower who sees each day as a gift, who discerns thin places in every circumstance, who soars, reveling in life's beauty. L. B. Cowman puts it well: "Strive to be one of the few who walk this earth with the ever present realization — every morning, noon, and night — that the unknown that people call heaven is directly behind those things that are visible."[10]

Let it be, sweet Jesus. Let it be.

Acknowledgments

Patrick, thanks for reading the raw parts of this manuscript and giving me permission to grieve and rejoice on the page.

D'Ann Mateer and Leslie Wilson: you help make my words sing. I'm indebted to you in the best sense.

Andy Meisenheimer, I appreciate your steady hand and present-tense advice as I worked through this manuscript.

Beth Jusino, more than a terrific agent, you're my friend.

Blessings upon my prayer team that prayed me through the heartache and triumph of this book: Kevin and Renee Bailey, Lilli Brenchley, Gahlen and Lee Ann Crawford, Jeanne Damoff, Pamela Dowd, Colleen Eslinger, Katy and Eric Gedney, Sandra Glahn, Jack and Helen Graves, Kim Griffith, Ed and Sue Harrell, Debbie Hutchison, Cyndi Kraweitz, Pam LeTourneau, Rae McIlrath, Michael and Renee Mills, Kim Moore, Marilyn Neel, Caroline O'Neill, Kathy O'Neill, Don Pape, Jen Powell, Brandy Prince, Katy Raymond, Marcia Robbins, Darren and Holly Sapp, Tom and Holly Schmidt, Carla Smith, Erin Teske, Jim and Stacey Tomisser, Heidi VanDyken, JR and Ginger Vassar, Rod and Mary Vestal, Tracy Walker, Jodie Westfall, Denise Wilhite, Betsy Williams, Jan Winebrenner, and Liz Wolf. Your prayers held me close to Jesus as I spent life in retrospect, and it's those prayers that will make the impact of this book eternal.

Jesus, You've met me in many a thin place, turning my trials into triumphs. Thank You. Thank You. Thank You.

Notes

1. Byron Hagan, Margaret Becker, and Michael Quinlan, "Cave It In," *Falling Forward*, EMI CMG Publishing, 1998. Used by permission.
2. Oswald Chambers, *My Utmost for His Highest* (Westwood, N.J.: Barbour, 2006), 49.
3. Mark Buchanan, *The Rest of God* (Nashville: Thomas Nelson, 2007), 210.
4. Anne Lamott, *Bird by Bird: Some Instructions on Writing and Life* (New York: Anchor Books, 1995), 226.
5. Dan Allender, *How Children Raise Parents* (Colorado Springs, Colo.: WaterBrook Press), 8.
6. Chambers, 59.
7. Chambers, 126.
8. *Anne of Avonlea* script, website: *http://greengables−2.tripod.com/script/2part9.html*.
9. Karen M. Thomas, "Family Lines and the Knots of Adoption," (Dallas, TX: *The Dallas Morning News*, April 18, 2007).
10. L. B. Cowman, *Streams in the Desert* (Grand Rapids: Zondervan, 2008), 288.

Daisy Chain
A Novel

Mary E. DeMuth

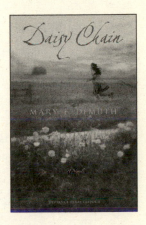

The abrupt disappearance of young Daisy Chance from a small Texas town in 1973 spins three lives out of control — Jed, whose guilt over not protecting his friend Daisy strangles him; Emory Chance, who blames her own choices for her daughter's demise; and Ouisie Pepper, who is plagued by headaches while pierced by the shattered pieces of a family in crisis.

In this first book in the Defiance, Texas Trilogy, fourteen-year-old Jed Pepper has a sickening secret: He's convinced it's his fault his best friend Daisy went missing. Jed's pain sends him on a quest for answers to mysteries woven through the fabric of his own life and the lives of the families of Defiance, Texas. When he finally confronts the terrible truths he's been denying all his life, Jed must choose between rebellion and love, anger and freedom.

Daisy Chain is an achingly beautiful southern coming-of-age story crafted by a bright new literary talent. It offers a haunting yet hopeful backdrop for human depravity and beauty, for terrible secrets and God's surprising redemption.

Softcover: 978-0-310-27836-8

Pick up a copy at your favorite bookstore or online!

A Slow Burn
A Novel

Mary E. DeMuth

"Beautifully and sensitively written, her characters realistic and well-developed. Mary DeMuth has a true gift for showing how God's light can penetrate even the darkest of situations."

— Chuck Colson

She touched Daisy's shoulder. So cold. So hard. So unlike Daisy. Yet so much like herself it made Emory shudder.

Burying her grief, Emory Chance is determined to find her daughter Daisy's murderer — a man she saw in a flicker of a vision. But when the investigation hits every dead end, her despair escalates. As questions surrounding Daisy's death continue to mount, Emory's safety is shattered by the pursuit of a stranger, and she can't shake the sickening fear that her own choices contributed to Daisy's disappearance. Will she ever experience the peace her heart longs for?

The second book in the Defiance, Texas Trilogy, this suspenseful novel is about courageous love, the burden of regret, and bonds that never break. It is about the beauty and the pain of telling the truth. Most of all, it is about the power of forgiveness and what remains when shame no longer holds us captive.

Softcover: 978-0-310-27837-5

DEFIANCE TEXAS TRILOGY — BOOK 3

Life in Defiance
A Novel

Mary E. DeMuth

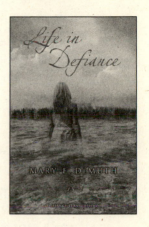

In a town she personifies, Ouisie Pepper wrestles with her own defiance. Desperate to become the wife and mother her husband Hap demands, Ouisie pours over a simple book about womanhood, constantly falling short, but determined to improve.

Through all that self-improvement, Ouisie carries a terrible secret: she knows who killed Daisy Chance. As her children inch closer to uncovering the killer's identity and Hap's rages roar louder and become increasingly violent, Ouisie has to make a decision. Will she protect her children by telling her secret? Or will Hap's violence silence them all?

Set on the backdrop of Defiance, Texas, Ouisie's journey typifies the choices we all face— whether to tell the truth about secrets and fight for the truth or bury them forever and live with the violent consequences.

Softcover: 978-0-310-27838-2

Pick up a copy at your favorite bookstore or online!

Share Your Thoughts

With the Author: Your comments will be forwarded to the author when you send them to *zauthor@zondervan.com*.

With Zondervan: Submit your review of this book by writing to *zreview@zondervan.com*.

Free Online Resources at
www.zondervan.com

Zondervan AuthorTracker: Be notified whenever your favorite authors publish new books, go on tour, or post an update about what's happening in their lives at www.zondervan.com/authortracker.

Daily Bible Verses and Devotions: Enrich your life with daily Bible verses or devotions that help you start every morning focused on God. Visit www.zondervan.com/newsletters.

Free Email Publications: Sign up for newsletters on Christian living, academic resources, church ministry, fiction, children's resources, and more. Visit www.zondervan.com/newsletters.

Zondervan Bible Search: Find and compare Bible passages in a variety of translations at www.zondervanbiblesearch.com.

Other Benefits: Register yourself to receive online benefits like coupons and special offers, or to participate in research.

ZONDERVAN®

ZONDERVAN.com/
AUTHORTRACKER
follow your favorite authors